United States
Department
of Agriculture

Forest Service

**Rocky Mountain
Research Station**

General Technical Report
RMRS-GTR-257

June 2011

A System for Assessing Vulnerability of Species (SAVS) to Climate Change

Karen E. Bagne, Megan M. Friggens, and Deborah M. Finch

I0447472

Bagne, Karen E.; Friggens, Megan M.; and Finch, Deborah M. 2011. **A System for Assessing Vulnerability of Species (SAVS) to Climate Change**. Gen. Tech. Rep. RMRS-GTR-257. Fort Collins, CO. U.S. Department of Agriculture, Forest Service, Rocky Mountain Research Station. 28 p.

Abstract

Sustained conservation of species requires integration of future climate change effects, but few tools exist to assist managers. The System for Assessing Vulnerability of Species (SAVS) identifies the relative vulnerability or resilience of vertebrate species to climate change. Designed for managers, the SAVS is an easily applied tool that uses a questionnaire of 22 predictive criteria to create vulnerability scores. The user scores species' attributes relating to potential vulnerability or resilience associated with projections for their region. Six scores are produced: an overall score denoting level of vulnerability or resilience, four categorical scores (habitat, physiology, phenology, and biotic interactions) indicating source of vulnerability, and an uncertainty score, which reflects user confidence in the predicted response. The SAVS provides a framework for integrating new information into the climate change assessment process.

Keywords: climate change, vulnerability, vertebrate species, conservation, resource management

Authors

Karen E. Bagne is an ecologist and wildlife biologist for the USFS Rocky Mountain Research Station.

Megan M. Friggens is a Research Ecologist (post doctoral) within the USFS Rocky Mountain Research Station.

Deborah M. Finch is the Program Manager for the Grassland, Shrubland and Desert program of the USFS Rocky Mountain Research Station.

Acknowledgments

Funding for this project was provided by the U.S. Forest Service (Climate Change Initiative), the U.S. Fish and Wildlife Service (Middle Rio Grande Bosque Improvement Initiative), The Nature Conservancy (Santa Fe Office), and the Department of Defense (Legacy Program). Sharon Coe, University of Arizona and Rocky Mountain Research Station; Bruce Young, NatureServe; and Molly Cross, Wildlife Conservation Society, provided manuscript review and discussion that improved this tool. Collaborators who inspired tool development include Carolyn Enquist and David Gori, The Nature Conservancy; Lisa Graumlich, University of Arizona; and Heather Bateman, Arizona State University Polytechnic. Further support and advice was provided by Jack Triepke and Bryce Rickels of US Forest Service, Region 3.

Contents

Cover Photos: Clockwise from top: Cactus Ferruginous Pygmy-Owl (*Glaucidium brasilianum cactorum*) courtesy of National Park Service; Northern Prairie Skink (*Eumeces septentrionalis septentrionalis*); Southwestern Willow Flycatcher (*Empidonax traillii extimus*) by Jim Rorabaugh, USFWS; Canada Lynx (*Lynx canadensis*) by Michael Zahra; American Pika (*Ochotona princeps*) from the Canadian Rocky Mountains by sevenstar; Desert Tortoise (*Gopherus agassizii*) courtesy of USGS.

A System for Assessing Vulnerability of Species (SAVS) to Climate Change

Karen E. Bagne, Megan M. Friggens, and Deborah M. Finch

Introduction

Global climate change is already affecting habitats and species worldwide (Root and others 2003; Enquist and Gori 2008). Yet we do not know how climate change will alter ecosystems because climate predictions are uncertain, global carbon and nitrogen cycling is complex, and our knowledge of ecological relationships is incomplete (Figure 1). It is clear, however, that warming trends will continue in the near future regardless of attempts to curtail greenhouse gas emissions (Caldeira and others 2003). Natural selection provides a mechanism whereby species can adapt to changes in their environments (Skelly and others 2007), but the speed with which climate is currently changing precludes adaptation in many species (Figure 2) (Janzen 1994; Visser 2008). Species unable to relocate or adapt to changing conditions will be at an increased risk of extinction. Additionally, climate projections vary regionally and effective strategies for conserving species under climate change need to integrate regional information on biogeography and ecology (Hannah and others 2002; Seavy and others 2008). The magnitude of the problem constitutes a major challenge for conservation practitioners. Despite these challenges, the potential impact on global biodiversity makes efforts to conserve species critically important.

Natural resource conservation is an iterative and adaptive process of identifying targets, implementing management actions, monitoring, and reviewing (Holling 1978; Walters and Holling 1990). Given the magnitude of the threat posed by climate change, the large number of species at risk, and the uncertainty of future conditions, conserving biodiversity in the future will rely on our ability to accurately identify targets and focus limited resources.

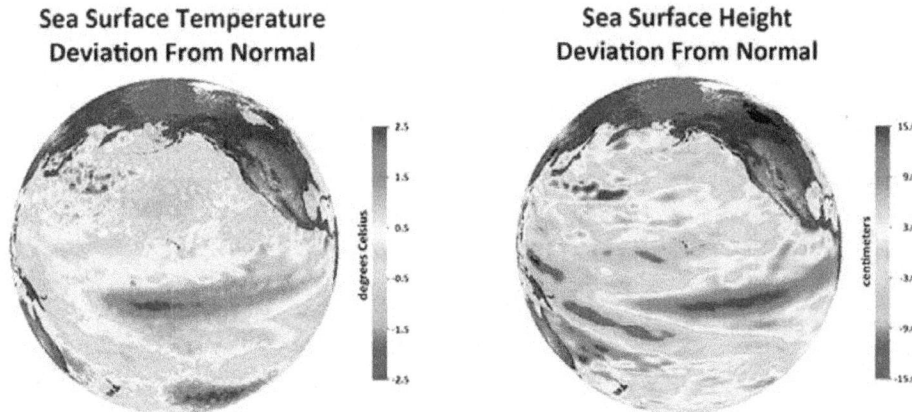

Sea Surface Temperature Deviation From Normal

Sea Surface Height Deviation From Normal

Figure 1. An example of one of the many consequences of climate change. This figure shows deviations from normal sea surface temperatures (left) and sea surface heights (right) at the peak of the 2009-2010 central Pacific El Niño, as measured by NOAA polar orbiting satellites and NASA's Jason-1 spacecraft, respectively. The warmest temperatures and highest sea levels were located in the central equatorial Pacific. This represents a relatively new type of El Niño in which warm waters are present in the central-equatorial Pacific Ocean, rather than in the eastern-equatorial Pacific. This type of El Nino is becoming more common and progressively stronger due to recent warming trends (Tong and McPhaden 2010). Image credit: NASA/JPL-NOAA.

USDA Forest Service Gen. Tech. Rep. RMRS-GTR-257. 2011

1

Figure 2. Shepard Glacier in Glacier National Park, Montana, as seen in 1913 (left) and 2005 (right). Image credit: USGS.

Assessments of vulnerability or extinction risk are valuable tools for identifying targets and prioritizing conservation needs so that management actions, or adaptation strategies, can be directed in an effective and efficient manner (Patt and others 2009; Glick and Stein 2011). Assessments that also identify how species, habitats, or ecosystems are affected by projected changes enable managers to develop new protocols and assess current management practices in light of expected future conditions (Füssel and Klein 2008; Glick and Stein 2011). In this paper, we describe a new System for Assessing Vulnerability of Species (SAVS) that identifies how and to what extent vertebrate species may be vulnerable to climate change (Table 1).

The SAVS is a simple and flexible tool designed for managers to assess the relative risk of individual species to population declines in response to projected changes in climate and related phenomena. The SAVS uses an easily completed questionnaire based on predictive criteria (Table 1) that translate response of terrestrial vertebrate species into scores indicating vulnerability or resilience to climate change. In addition to the scoring tool itself (Table 1), we provide worksheets for score calculations (Box 1), methods for calculating uncertainty (Box 1), detailed instructions for scoring a species (Appendix 1), guidelines for tool application, a glossary of terms, and discussion of application of scores to vulnerability assessments.

Development of SAVS

Scoring Strategy

Our goal was to create a tool that predicts the likelihood and direction of population change for individual species under future climate scenarios. Although we focused on identifying vulnerable species (those with a high likelihood of negative population change) we also considered characteristics associated with resilience as not all species will respond negatively to climate change (Araújo and others 2006). Response to climate change is estimated in SAVS as the cumulative value of a set of predictors of population change that represent negative or positive response to climate change. This cumulative score increases with increasing vulnerability with the range of estimated scores that create a standard for comparison among species. The SAVS is designed to be applied by the user to a targeted region and time period encompassing a uniform set of climate predictions (e.g., a single climate zone), although we did integrate the use of additional climate information for migratory species. The SAVS focuses on the effects of climate change rather than integrating threats from other sources, because current management or conservation plans generally cover those topics. To reduce complexity, this version of SAVS applies only to terrestrial vertebrate species.

Response of species to climate change is predicted from characteristics associated with exposure, sensitivity, or adaptive capacity (Glick and Stein 2011; IPCC 2007) (Table 2). Exposure refers to the degree to which a species will experience changing climate and conditions, whereas sensitivity is the degree to which a species is actually affected by those conditions (Glick and Stein 2011). Adaptive capacity is the potential for a species to reduce exposure or sensitivity (Glick and Stein 2011). We used basic ecological principles and published studies linking survival or reproduction to climate or related phenomena (e.g., fire, floods, snowpack levels) to identify characteristics or traits indicative of sensitivity or adaptive capacity.

2

USDA Forest Service Gen. Tech. Rep. RMRS-GTR-257. 2011

Table 1. The System for Assessing Vulnerability of Species (SAVS) (v.2.0): A Climate Change Tool for Resource Managers. Download from http://www.fs.fed.us/rmrs/species-vulnerability/.

Habitat

H1.   Area and distribution: breeding. Is the area or location of the associated vegetation type used for breeding activities by this species expected to change? Specific habitat elements and food resources are considered in other questions.

    a.   Area used for breeding habitat expected to decline or shift from current location (SCORE = 1)

    b.   Area used for breeding habitat expected to stay the same and in approximately the same location (SCORE = 0)

    c.   Area used for breeding habitat expected to increase and include the current location (SCORE = -1)

H2.   Area and distribution: non-breeding. Is the area or location of the associated vegetation type used for non-breeding activities by this species expected to change?

    a   Area used for non-breeding habitat expected to decline or shift from current location (SCORE = 1)

    b.   Area used for non-breeding habitat expected to stay the same in approximately the same location (SCORE = 0)

    c.   Area used for non-breeding habitat expected to increase and include the current location (SCORE = -1)

H3.   Habitat components: breeding. Are specific habitat components required for breeding expected to change within the associated vegetation type?

    a.   Required breeding habitat components expected to decrease (SCORE = 1)

    b.   Required breeding habitat components unlikely to change OR habitat components required for breeding unknown (SCORE = 0)

    c.   Required breeding habitat components expected to increase (SCORE = -1)

H4.   Habitat components: non-breeding. Are other specific habitat components required for survival during non-breeding periods expected to change within the associated vegetation type?

    a.   Required non-breeding habitat components expected to decrease (SCORE = 1)

    b.   Required non-breeding habitat components unlikely to change OR habitat components required for breeding unknown (SCORE = 0)

    c.   Required non-breeding habitat components expected to increase (SCORE = -1)

H5.   Habitat quality. Within habitats occupied, are features of the habitat associated with better reproductive success or survival expected to change?

    a.   Projected changes are likely to negatively affect habitat features associated with improved reproductive success or survival (SCORE = 1)

    b.   Projected changes are unlikely to affect habitat features associated with improved reproductive success or survival (SCORE = 0)

    c.   Projected changes are likely to positively affect habitat features associated with improved reproductive success or survival (SCORE = -1)

H6.   Ability to colonize new areas. What is the potential for this species to disperse?

    a.   Low ability to disperse (SCORE = 1)

    b.   Mobile, but dispersal is sex-biased (only one sex disperses) (SCORE = 0)

    c.   Very mobile, both sexes disperse (SCORE = -1)

H7.   Migratory or transitional habitats. Does this species require additional habitats during migration that are separated from breeding and non-breeding habitats?

    Additional habitats required that are separated from breeding and non-breeding habitats (e.g., most migratory species) (SCORE = 1)

    No additional habitats required that are separated from breeding and non-breeding habitats (e.g., most resident species and short-distance migrants) (SCORE = 0)

Physiology

PS1.   Physiological thresholds. Are limiting physiological conditions expected to change?

    a.   Projected changes in temperature and moisture are likely to exceed upper physiological thresholds (e.g., activities occur in very hot climates, amphibians in drier climates, species with narrow thermal range) (SCORE = 1)

(con.)

Table 1. (continued).

b. Projected changes in temperature or moisture will primarily remain within physiological thresholds OR species is inactive during limiting conditions (e.g., species with moderate thermal range, aestivators that avoid hot/dry conditions) (SCORE = 0)

c. Projected changes in temperature or moisture will decrease current incidents where lower thresholds are exceeded (e.g., species active in very cold climates, amphibians in wetter climates, species with very broad thermal range) (SCORE = -1)

PS2. Sex ratio. Is sex ratio determined by temperature?

    a   Yes. (SCORE = 1)

    b. No. (SCORE = 0)

PS3. Exposure to weather-related disturbance. Are disturbance events (e.g., severe storms, fires, floods) that affect survival or reproduction expected to change?

a. Projected changes in disturbance events will likely decrease survival or reproduction (SCORE = 1)

b. Survival and reproduction are not strongly affected by disturbance events OR disturbance events are not expected to change (SCORE = 0)

c. Projected changes in disturbance events will likely increase survival or reproduction (SCORE = -1)

PS4. Limitations to daily activity period. Are projected temperature or precipitation regimes that influence activity period of species expected to change?

a. Duration of daily active periods likely to be reduced (e.g., heliotherms in hot climates, terrestrial amphibians in drier climates) (SCORE = 1)

b. Duration of daily active periods unchanged or not limited by climate (species in habitats buffered from extremes, nocturnal species, primarily aquatic amphibians) (SCORE = 0)

c. Duration of daily active periods likely to increase (e.g., heliotherms in cool climates, terrestrial amphibians in wetter climates) (SCORE = -1)

PS5. Survival during resource fluctuation. Does this species have flexible strategies to cope with variation in resources across multiple years?

a. Species has no flexible strategies to cope with variable resources across multiple years (SCORE = 1)

b. Species has flexible strategies to cope with variable resources across multiple years (e.g., alternative life forms, irruptive, explosive breeding, cooperative breeding) (SCORE = -1)

PS6. Energy requirements. What is this species' metabolic rate?

a. Very high metabolic rates (e.g., shrews, hummingbirds) (SCORE = 1)

b. Moderate (e.g., most endotherms) (SCORE = 0)

c. Low (i.e. ectotherms) (SCORE = -1)

Phenology

PH1. Mismatch potential: Cues. Does this species use temperature or moisture cues to initiate activities related to fecundity or survival (e.g., hibernation, migration, breeding)?

a. Species primarily uses temperature or moisture cues to initiate activities (e.g., some hibernators, aestivators, rainfall breeders) (SCORE = 1)

b. Species does not primarily use temperature or moisture cues OR no cues to predict or initiate activities (e.g., photoperiod or circadian rhythms, resource levels) (SCORE = 0)

PH2. Mismatch potential: Event timing. Are activities related to species' fecundity or survival tied to discrete resource peaks (e.g., food, breeding sites) that are expected to change?

a. Species' fitness is tied to discrete resource peaks that are expected to change (SCORE = 1)

b. Species' fitness is tied to discrete resource peaks that are NOT expected to change (SCORE = 0)

c. No temporal variation in resources or breeds year-round (SCORE = -1)

(con.)

Table 1. (continued).

PH3. Mismatch potential: Proximity. What is the separation in time or space between cues that initiate activities related to survival or fecundity and discrete events that provide critical resources?

    a. Critical resource occurs far in advance or in distant locations from cues or initiation of activity (SCORE = 1)

    b. Critical resource does NOT occur far in advance or in distant locations from cues or initiation of activity (SCORE =0)

    c. Species initiates activities directly from critical resource availability (e.g., opportunistic breeders) (SCORE = -1)

PH4. Resilience to timing mismatch. Does this species have more than one opportunity to time reproduction to important events?

    a. Species reproduces once per year or less (SCORE = 1)

    b. Species reproduces more than once per year (SCORE = -1)

Biotic Interactions

I1. Food resources. Are important food resources for this species expected to change?

    a. Primary food source(s) are expected to be negatively impacted by projected changes (SCORE = 1)

    b. Species consumes variety of prey/forage species OR primary food resource(s) not expected to be impacted by projected changes (SCORE =0)

    c. Primary food resource(s) expected to be positively impacted by projected changes (SCORE = -1)

I2. Predators. Are important predator populations for this species expected to change?

    a. Primary predator(s) are expected to be positively impacted by projected changes (SCORE = 1)

    b. Preyed upon by a suite of predators OR the primary predator is not expected to be impacted by projected changes (SCORE = 0)

    c. Species has no predators (SCORE = 0)

    d. Primary predator(s) expected to be negatively impacted by projected changes (SCORE = -1)

I3. Symbionts. Are populations of symbiotic species expected to change?

    a. Symbiotic species populations expected to be negatively impacted by projected changes (SCORE = 1)

    b. Symbiotic species populations not expected to be impacted by projected changes (SCORE = 0)

    c. No symbionts (SCORE =0)

    d. Symbiotic species populations expected to be positively impacted by projected changes (SCORE = -1)

I4. Disease. Is prevalence of diseases known to cause widespread mortality or reproductive failure in this species expected to change?

    a. Disease prevalence is expected to increase with projected changes (SCORE = 1)

    b. No known effects of expected changes on disease prevalence (SCORE = 0)

    c. Disease prevalence is expected to decrease with projected changes (SCORE = -1)

I5. Competitors. Are populations of important competing species expected to change?

    a. Major competitor species are expected to be positively impacted by projected changes (SCORE = 1)

    b. Species has a variety of competitive relationships OR no expected impacts of projected changes in major competitor species (SCORE = 0)

    c. Competing species are expected to be negatively impacted by projected changes (SCORE = -1)

Box 1. Computing Scores

Vulnerability

Positive values indicate vulnerability to climate change and negative scores indicate resilience. Factors are adjusted for max score per factor = 5 or -5 to aid comparison among factors. Overall scores are computed from all predictive criteria (i.e. the 22 questions) regardless of factor and adjusted for maximum score of 20 or a minimum score of -20. To calculate vulnerability scores, take the sum of positive values and the sum of negative values for each category and for all questions and use those values in the following equations:

Habitat Vulnerability = (Positive total x [5/7]) + (Negative total x [5/6])
Physiology Vulnerability = (Positive total x [5/6]) + (Negative total x [1])
Phenology Vulnerability = (Positive total x [5/4]) + (Negative total x [5/3])
Biotic Interaction Vulnerability = (Positive total x [1]) + (Negative total x [1])

Overall Vulnerability Score = (Positive total x [20/22]) + (Negative total x [20/19])

Uncertainty

Assuming climate change projections are correct, note the amount of information available for each question for assigning scores. Chose one of the following for each question:

a. Adequate information available to assign score for this species. SCORE = 0
b. Information is not adequate to confidently assign score OR conflicting predictions or responses make scoring difficult. SCORE = 1

Calculations are the percentage of uncertain scores for each factor and for all criteria (i.e., overall). Use the worksheet below to aid calculation. Calculate percent uncertainty using the equations below:

Percent uncertainty for Habitat = (Sum of uncertainty scores / 7)
Percent uncertainty for Physiology = (Sum of uncertainty scores / 6)
Percent uncertainty for Phenology = (Sum of uncertainty scores / 4)
Percent uncertainty for Interactions = (Sum of uncertainty scores / 5)

Percent of overall uncertainty = (Sum of uncertainty scores for all questions / 22)

Table 2. Criteria used in SAVS climate change tool address one or more of the three aspects of vulnerability as defined by the IPCC (2007). Each criterion represents an area expected to experience climate-related impacts.

Factor & Criteria		Vulnerability Component
Habitat		
H1.	Breeding habitat area and distribution	Exposure, Sensitivity
H1.	Non-breeding habitat area and distribution	Exposure, Sensitivity
H1.	Habitat components required for breeding	Exposure, Sensitivity
H1.	Habitat components required outside breeding	Exposure, Sensitivity
H1.	Habitat quality	Exposure, Sensitivity
H1.	Ability to colonize new areas	Adaptive Capacity
H1.	Reliance on migratory or transitional habitats	Sensitivity
Physiology		
PS1.	Physiological thresholds	Sensitivity, Adaptive Capacity
PS1.	Sex ratio related to temperature	Sensitivity
PS1.	Exposure to weather-related disturbance	Sensitivity, Exposure
PS1.	Changes to daily activity period	Sensitivity, Adaptive Capacity
PS1.	Survival during resource fluctuation	Adaptive Capacity
PS1.	Energy requirements	Sensitivity
Phenology		
PH1.	Mismatch potential: Cues	Sensitivity
PH1.	Mismatch potential: Event timing	Sensitivity
PH1.	Mismatch potential: Proximity	Sensitivity
PH1.	Resilience to timing mismatch	Sensitivity, Adaptive Capacity
Biotic Interactions		
I1.	Food resources	Exposure, Sensitivity
I2.	Predators	Exposure, Sensitivity
I3.	Symbionts	Exposure, Sensitivity
I4.	Disease	Exposure, Sensitivity
I5.	Competitors	Exposure, Sensitivity

We then integrated these traits with exposure to develop criteria predictive of climate change response into a scoring system that is regional and species specific (Table 1). Thus, scores include both the predicted climate-related change (e.g., increased burning) and the predicted response of the species (e.g., fire increases preferred habitat). The user obtains information on exposure before scoring from available climate projections for the target region (Table 3).

While developing the SAVS, we considered repeatability, relation to quantitative values, and independence from other scoring criteria (Beissinger and others 2000). To increase repeatability, each predictive criteria or question assesses anticipated negative, positive, or neutral impacts, but not degree of vulnerability. Because knowledge of species and climate change is incomplete, we designed the tool to be flexible to new information as well as a variety of information sources including published materials, personal knowledge, and expert consultation.

Scoring Criteria

We considered criteria based on published species' responses, observed or modeled, that could be used to predict direction, positive or negative, of climate change response. We identified a wide range of criteria that represent both direct and indirect responses to changes in temperature and precipitation, as well as to extreme events, which are important in driving population dynamics and natural selection (Boag and Grant 1984; Easterling and others 2000; Parmesan and others 2000). We selected criteria predictive of species response to climate change from four broad factors or categories: habitat, physiology, phenology, and biotic interactions.

Habitat—Predicted changes to global temperature and precipitation patterns will, consequently, alter habitats (McCarty 2001; Hitch and Leberg 2007; Sekercioglu and others 2008). We identified five criteria predictive

USDA Forest Service Gen. Tech. Rep. RMRS-GTR-257. 2011

7

Table 3. A list of the major types of data that should be gathered for SAVS. The questions addressed by the data are indicated in parentheses after the list item.

Climate Change Scenarios (all questions)
- Change in total annual precipitation
- Change in seasonal precipitation
- Change in average temperatures (night and day)
- Maximum summer temperatures
- Minimum winter temperatures
- Changes to snowpack duration, amount
- Change to number of frost days
- Projected drought duration and frequency
- Changes in potential, frequency and timing of flooding
- Changes in frequency, severity, extent or timing of fire disturbances
- Changes in frequency, duration, extent or timing of extreme weather events (e.g., storms, heat waves)

Natural History Data Needed for Species Assessments:

Habitat

Climate projections related to vegetation type for breeding and non-breeding habitats including disturbance processes (All Questions)

Habitat/associated vegetation type: Breeding and nonbreeding habitats, vegetation type associations (Questions 1, 2)

Habitat components required for breeding or survival (Questions 3, 4)

Any aspect of the breeding or nonbreeding habitat associated with habitat quality (improved breeding or survival) (Question 5)

Dispersal ability and sex biased dispersal (Question 6)

Migration habits/requirements (Question 7)

Physiology

Threshold or sensitivity to moisture or temperature extremes (Alternative: species range relative to area under assessment) (Question 1)

Sex ratio/temperature relationships (some reptiles) (Question 2)

Potential exposure of species to extreme weather condition/Known cases of mortality of failed reproduction related to weather events (Question 3)

Climate or weather-mediated limitations to active periods (Question 4)

Endothermic or exothermic (Question 5)

Variable life history strategies/Able to postpone reproductive output (Question 6)

Phenology

Temperature or moisture variables used as cues (Question 1)

Events that need to be timed to coincide with reproduction/survival (insect emergence, etc.) (Question 2)

Proximity (temporal and geographical) of cues, activities, and essential resources (Question 3)

Number of breeding attempts per year (Question 4)

Biotic Interactions

Identify primary food resources, expected changes to resources (Question 1)

Identify primary predators and expected changes to predator populations (Question 2)

Identify symbionts and expected changes to symbiont populations (Question 3)

Identify significant pathogen entities, disease risk factors, and expected changes to these issues (Question 4)

Identify major competitors and expected changes to competitor populations (Question 5)

8

USDA Forest Service Gen. Tech. Rep. RMRS-GTR-257. 2011

of population change as climate affects habitats: changes in habitat area or location, effects on habitat elements, changes in habitat quality, dispersal ability, and reliance on additional habitats during migration. We consider breeding and non-breeding habitats separately in this assessment, because requirements or locations for these activities differ for many species.

Survival is typically tied to specific habitats, which in turn are tied to local climate conditions. Thus, populations are likely to be affected as changes in local conditions change the availability of suitable habitat. In addition to changes in overall area, climate changes may result in major shifts in distribution of associated vegetation types. This also affects habitat availability, because of complexities arising from species-specific plant responses to climate and differences in new site characteristics such as soil profiles, existent vegetation, topography, and land use (Martínez-Meyer 2005; Ibáñez and others 2008). Significant shifts have been predicted for many vegetation types, including North American forests (Iverson and Prasad 2001; Rehfeldt and others 2006) and European alpine (Dirnböck and others 2003). We have already seen habitat loss for range-restricted species, such as those from high altitudes and distributional shifts (Figure 3) consistent with those predicted by warmer temperatures, and these responses are likely to increase as temperatures continue to rise (Root and others 2003; Parmesan 2006).

Species may also require additional features or components within suitable vegetation types for survival or reproduction. Climate changes can affect the availability of key ephemeral resources and critical habitat features. For example, the hydroperiod of amphibian breeding ponds is a critical component directly affected by changes in precipitation patterns (Paton and Crouch 2002). Populations of cavity-nesting birds are often affected by the availability of cavities (reviewed by Newton 1994) components potentially altered by climate change.

We can expect climate-induced changes to habitat quality when climate alters the structure or composition of habitat components that affect rates of survival or reproduction (Figure 4). For example, precipitation is closely associated with plant biomass, an important element of habitat quality for herbivores (Chase and others 2000). Habitat changes may also be related to snowpack and ice formation or sea level rise. Deeper snowpack is expected to hinder grazing animals in winter (Post and Stenseth 1999). Conversely, a smaller snowpack is expected to negatively affect species, such as lemmings and pikas that rely on snow for protection (Lindström 1994; Coulson and Malo 2008).

As habitats change, dispersal strategies and mobility of organisms become important indicators of how a species could cope with shifting habitats (Thomas and others 2004; Araújo and others 2006; Jiguet and others 2007). Species that are able to travel long distances have a greater chance of finding and colonizing new habitat patches. Conversely, some long distance dispersers are at an increased risk for negative habitat effects if they rely on multiple habitats that are likely to be exposed to disparate climate change effects (Visser and others 2008).

Figure 3. Over the last few decades the range of the Red Fox (right) has expanded northward and upward, displacing the Arctic Fox (left) in North American Tundra Habitat (Hersteinsson and MacDonald 1992). Boundary changes were related to warming trends, which increased food availability for the competitively superior Red Fox. In the context of the criteria used in the SAVS, warming is effectively increasing the area of suitable habitat for the Red Fox, a positive habitat effect, but increasing competitive pressure for the Arctic Fox, a negative interaction effect. Image credit: USGS and John Sarvis, USFWS.

USDA Forest Service Gen. Tech. Rep. RMRS-GTR-257. 2011

9

Figure 4. Increased snowpack can reduce access to forage during winter months and result in population declines in large ungulate species like these Caribou (Adamczewski and others 1988; Post and Stenseth 1999). Image credit: USGS.

Physiology—Species exhibit physiological requirements and limitations related to temperature and moisture (McCain 2007), which can help predict future impacts (Helmuth and others 2005). We identified six predictive criteria related to physiology: physiological thresholds, temperature-dependent sex ratios, exposure to extreme climate or disturbance events, energetics related to activity patterns, adaptations to cope with resource fluctuations, and capacity to moderate metabolic expenditure.

The range of temperature and moisture tolerances exhibited by species is important in predicting direct impacts of climate (Beever and others 2003; Humphries and others 2004; Bernardo and Spotila 2006). For birds in France, species that had a lower tolerance for high temperatures were more likely to have experienced recent declines (Jiguet et al. 2007). Additionally, nocturnal reptiles and small mammals generally have lower tolerances for high temperatures than diurnal species (Cowles 1940). A comparison of metabolic stress in montane salamanders along an elevational gradient indicated that species that adapted to cool temperatures were physiologically intolerant of increasing temperatures (Bernardo and Spotila 2006). Conversely, species that tolerate extremely warm or dry conditions are not necessarily more tolerant of climate change, but rather may be vulnerable to temperature increases if they are already near their physiological limits (Figure 5) (Hargrove 2010).

Some reptiles have temperature-sensitive sex determination and will be vulnerable to skewed sex ratios that ultimately affect population viability (Janzen 1994; Mitchell and others 2008). For example, mean temperature increases of 4 °C are projected to eliminate males in painted turtle populations (Janzen 1994).

Disturbance and extreme conditions affect species' distributions and drive natural selection (Boag and Grant 1984; Parmesan and others 2000). Changes in climate-related disturbance events, such as fire, flooding, or freeze events are expected to affect species survival and reproduction (Westerling and others 2006; Hamlet and Lettenmaier 2007). Some bird species are exposed to storms and hurricanes during migration and could be affected if these events intensify or become more frequent (Butler 2000; Frederiksen and others 2008). Breeding success of Humboldt penguins, which nest in burrows or on the ground, is negatively impacted by flooding caused by events such as the heavy rains associated with El Niño events (Simeone and others 2002). Response to disturbance events, however, can vary depending on a species' sensitivity (Pike and Stiner 2007). For example, some bird species are adapted to take advantage of post-fire habitats, while others favor habitats in later stages of succession (Hutto 2008; Bagne and Purcell 2009).

In addition to physiological thresholds, energetic constraints linked with climate will play an important role in species' response. Population variations and reproductive output are often associated with energetic tradeoffs related to climate (Franklin and others 2000). Even moderate changes to daily temperature or humidity levels can influence daily activity patterns and ultimately limit food intake, limit access to mates, or increase predation risk (Lueth 1941; Walsberg 2000; Sinervo and others 2010). Recent local extinctions in Mexican lizards were attributed to climate-induced changes to suitable foraging time (Sinervo and others 2010). Alternatively, changes in limiting conditions may decrease restrictions for some species. Warmer

Figure 5. Desert adapted species are also likely to be sensitive to climate change. The distribution of 28 bird species in California moved an average of 116 m upslope over a 26-year period corresponding to temperature increases (Hargrove 2010). While species like the California Quail (left) showed substantial movement up slope, others like the black throated sparrow (right) showed no movement despite significant reductions in breeding success at lower elevation sites relative to upland areas. Such observations indicate that adaption to arid conditions is not by itself an indicator of resilience to future climate changes. Image credit: Sid Mosdell and Elaine R. Wilson, Wikimedia Commons.

conditions in the Arctic are expected to improve energetic conditions for hibernating mammal species in that region (Humphries and others 2004).

Warming is expected to increase climate variability (IPCC 2007) and affect the availability of resources and habitat conditions needed for species survival and reproduction. Increasing unpredictability in weather conditions may favor species with life history traits that allow them to endure and recover from periods of drought, excessive heat, or other limiting conditions (Bronson 2009). Some species have specific adaptations or strategies that allow them to cope with fluctuating resources (Figure 6). For example, spadefoot toad tadpoles can switch between omnivore and carnivore morphs in response to variation in pond longevity and food abundance, allowing them to maximize recruitment under a variety of conditions (Pfennig 1992). Cooperative breeding (Ligon and Burt 2004) and irruptive movements are also thought to be adaptations to cope with unstable food supplies (Newton 2006).

Ectothermic animals, which have lower resting metabolic rates than birds or mammals, might also have a survival advantage over endotherms when resources are restricted (Bennett and Ruben 1979).

Figure 6. A Couch's Spadefoot Toad from Amistad National Recreational Area, Texas. Like most amphibians, these toads rely on water for fertilization and tadpole development and are therefore sensitive to the availability of appropriate ponds. However, these species also have adaptations that may allow them to better survive future climate conditions including the capacity to aestivate, sometimes for several years, during dry periods and polymorphic tadpole forms (see text). Image credit: Clinton and Charles Robertson, Wikimedia Commons.

USDA Forest Service Gen. Tech. Rep. RMRS-GTR-257. 2011

11

Phenology—Effects of climate change on phenology are among the best known (McCarty 2001). Many species improve survival and reproduction by timing important biological activities like reproduction, migration, and hibernation to seasonal variations in resources and habitat conditions. These species initiate activities in response to cues that directly, or indirectly, signal favorable resource events or environmental conditions. We identified four phenological criteria: reliance on climate-related cues, reliance on distinctly timed resource events, proximity of cues to events, and the potential for synchrony of breeding and favorable conditions

Changes in temperature and precipitation alter the timing of life history events through altering cues, altering the benefits associated with the cue or both (Beebee 1995, Dunn and Winkler 1999). When cues become disassociated from their benefits, populations can be reduced (Both and others 2006). Earlier flowering (Bowers 2007), breeding (Millar and Herdman 2004; Parmesan 2007), and migration (Bradley and others 1999) have been linked to climate change. As different species respond to changing temperatures at different rates, the risk of mistiming of resource peaks within and across ecosystems is increased. For other species, mismatch occurs when unchanging endogenous cues lead to timed behaviors that no longer correspond to critical resources that track climate changes (Inouye and others 2000; Carey 2009). For example, timing of migration in Nearctic-Neotropical birds is primarily endogenous (Hagan and others 1991), thus increasing the potential for mismatches in timing with temperature sensitive resources on the breeding grounds (Figure 7). Changes in the timing of favorable sea ice conditions without accompanying changes to breeding timing have greatly reduced emperor penguin populations with probable extinction if penguins fail to adapt (Jenouvrier and others 2009). For the purpose of this assessment, we assumed vulnerability increases with any expected shifts in the timing of either cues or associated events (Root and others 2003), but acknowledge that synchrony may be maintained when timing shifts of interacting elements respond equally and, thus, continue to coincide.

Some species are better able to adjust to changes in the timing of discrete events or conditions. Opportunistic or eruptive breeders respond rapidly to irregular events and may be less prone to mistiming (Visser and others 2004). Similarly, species with more than one breeding attempt per year or that have extended breeding periods are more likely to experience synchrony with critical resources or conditions in any given year (Jiguet and others 2007).

Biotic Interactions—Climate change has the potential to indirectly affect many species where species are

Figure 7. The European Pied Flycatcher is a well known example of how climate change can influence populations through the mismatch of timed events (Both and others 2006). This long distance migrant has experienced populations declines of 90% where warmer temperatures have led to earlier peaks in food resources on breeding grounds. These declines are not seen for populations that migrate to areas where food resources continue to peak later in the season. Image credit: Caricata de Aelwyn, Wikimedia Commons.

closely associated through trophic or other interactions (Memmott and others 2007). Climate change will have the most severe consequences for the stability and persistence of biotic communities when multiple or critical (e.g., keystone) species are negatively impacted. We selected five primary interactions—food, predation, symbiosis, disease, and competition—as the most important indicators of a species' ultimate climate change response. Although an oversimplification of ecological relationships, these interactions encompass major aspects of life history that are feasible to include in a simple scoring tool.

Availability of food resources directly impacts survival and reproduction. In general, specialist species that rely on one or only a few other species for food are considered at greater risk of extinction because they are more sensitive to stochastic events that change food availability (Gilg and others 2009; Gilman and others 2010). Similarly, changes in the population of predators as a result of climate change

12

USDA Forest Service Gen. Tech. Rep. RMRS-GTR-257. 2011

could have striking downstream effects on prey species. Climate has already influenced predator-prey interactions through effects on both the survival (Barton and Schmitz 2009) and hunting efficiency of predators (Schmitz and others 2003). Disease exposure may be altered if climate becomes more, or less, favorable to vectors (Figure 8) (Benning and others 2002; Freed and others 2005). A number of studies relate the recent emergence and re-emergence of many wildlife diseases to the effects of warming trends on vector species (Githeko and others 2000; Epstein 2001; Harvell and others 2002) as well as host immunity (Rohr and Raffel 2010). Climate-related disruptions to plant-pollinator interactions and mutualisms have profound implications for ecosystem function (Gilman and others 2010; Memmott and others 2007). Competitive interactions can also be altered as new climate regimes favor or hinder competitors (Brown and others 1997; Jackson and others 2009; Gilman and others 2010). Many non-native invasive species are expected to have a competitive advantage under future climate with potential consequences for native species (Carroll 2007).

Application of SAVS

Scoring Species

To begin scoring a species, the user selects a target region and time period for climate change projections that is relevant to management goals. The targeted region can be a management unit, an ecoregion, or the entire range of species, but the boundaries for a set of scores cannot encompass disparate climate projections (i.e., multiple estimates of exposure). Once selected, the user collects information on projected temperature and precipitation as well as related phenomena such as snowpack, sea level, and disturbance for the target area (Table 3). Additional projections are also collected for migratory species. Next, the user collects data on the species to be scored from literature or expert sources (Table 3). Using this data, the user selects among the options for each question and marks a value for uncertainty. Responses relating to situations where a species is expected to benefit from future conditions either by possessing a favorable trait or through an expectation for favorable conditions have a value of -1 and signify resilience. Responses relating to expectations of less favorable situations for a species because it either possesses a trait that confers greater sensitivity or is expected to be exposed to declining conditions have a value of +1 and signify vulnerability. Both responses to questions and uncertainty values are tallied and scores calculated using the formulas presented in Box 1. Users can access a web-based version of SAVS (http://www.fs.fed.us/rmrs/species-vulnerability/) or use the scoring worksheet in Table 4 and Box 1 to calculate scores by hand.

Uncertainty Scores—It is difficult to incorporate climate change into vulnerability assessments, because the strongest climate change effects have yet to manifest, effects are known for relatively few species, and future predictions are inherently complex. The complexity of ecological communities is also likely to lead to unpredictable changes relating to the formation of new species assemblages (Brown and others 1997) and novel ecosystems (Harris and others 2006). For this reason,

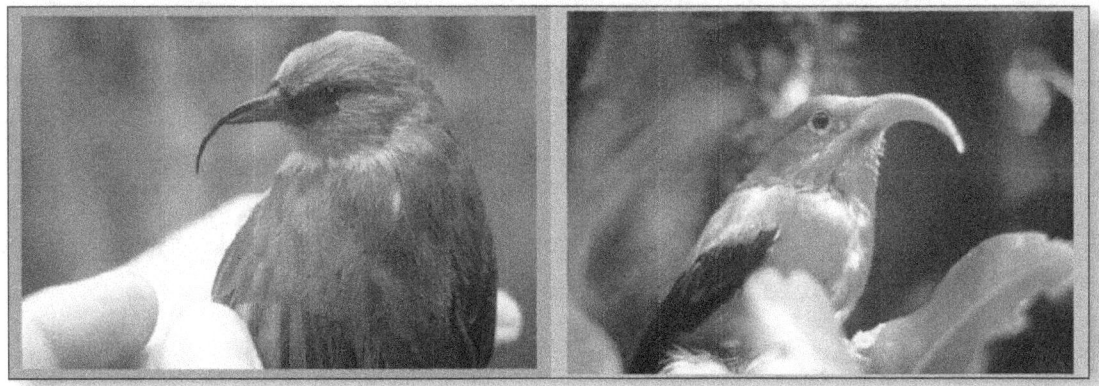

Figure 8. Avian malaria poses a threat to many bird species endemic to Hawaii. Malaria transmission is highly dependent upon climate conditions and has so far been restricted to the mid elevation zones that support the mosquito vector. Both the Akiapola'au (left) and 'I'iwi (right) survive in high elevation refuges on Kauai, Maui, and Hawaii. However, warmer temperatures would favor the expansion of mosquitoes into higher elevations and result in a loss of 60-90% of these high elevation refuges (Atkinson and LaPointe 2009). Temperature changes will also extend the season for disease transmission, potentially leaving bird populations with no period for recovery. Image credit: USFWS.

USDA Forest Service Gen. Tech. Rep. RMRS-GTR-257. 2011

13

Table 4. Scoring Worksheet. Mark the corresponding boxes for the selected score and for uncertainty. Use Box 1 to calculate scores. Shaded cells are not valid scores. Questions have been abbreviated.

	Vulnerability			Uncertainty	
HABITAT	**A (1)**	**B (0)**	**C (-1)**	**A (yes)**	**B (no)**
H1. Is the area or location of the general associated vegetation type used for breeding activities by this species expected to change?					
H2. Is the area or location of the general associated vegetation type used for non-breeding activities by this species expected to change?					
H3. Are specific habitat components required for breeding expected to change within associated vegetation type?					
H4. Are specific habitat components required for survival expected to change within associated vegetation type?					
H5. Within habitats occupied, are features of the habitat associated with better reproductive success or survival expected to change?					
H6. What is the potential for this species to disperse?					
H7. Does this species require additional distinct habitats during migration?					
	Total columns			Total "yes"	
Enter Here ->					
PHYSIOLOGY	**1**	**0**	**-1**	**A (yes)**	**B (no)**
PS1. Are limiting physiological conditions expected to change?					
PS2. Is sex ratio determined by temperature?					
PS3. Are disturbance events that affect survival or reproduction expected to change?					
PS4. Is activity period expected to change?					
PS5. Does this species employ adaptive strategies?					
PS6. What is this species metabolic rate?					
	Total columns			Total "yes"	
Enter Here ->					
PHENOLOGY	**1**	**0**	**-1**	**A (yes)**	**B (no)**
PH1. Does this species use temperature or moisture cues to initiate activities?					
PH2. Are activities tied to discrete resource peaks that are expected to change?					
PH3. What is the separation between cues/activities and discrete events/ resources?					
PH4. Does this species have more than one reproduction event per year?					
	Total columns			Total "yes"	
Enter Here ->					
INTERACTIONS	**1**	**0**	**-1**	**A (yes)**	**B (no)**
I1. Are important food resources for this species expected to change?					
I2. Are important predator populations expected to change?					
I3. Are populations of symbiotic species expected to change?					
I4. Is prevalence of disease in this species expected to change?					
I5. Are populations of important competing species expected to change?					
	Total columns			Total "yes"	
Enter Here ->					

SAVS includes uncertainty scores to identify specific areas where scoring was complicated by multiple effects, predictions, interactions, or a general lack of data. An uncertainty score is calculated for each criterion or question and used to assess overall confidence in the predicted species' response (Box 1). Uncertainty is quantified as the percentage of criterion scored where either the direction of change could not be predicted because of lack of information or the predicted response was comprised of both negative and positive aspects.

Interpreting Scores—The scoring system outputs four factor scores and an overall score for a species within the targeted region and time period. Overall scores and factor scores are calculated differently and are used for different purposes as detailed in the next section. The number of criteria is unequal among the four factors (Table 1). Thus, to facilitate comparison among factors, we adjusted these scores by the number of questions present in that factor. Calculations for the overall score treat all criteria as equal predictors of vulnerability or resilience and, therefore, are not simply the sum of the factor scores.

When the scores associated with each response are tallied, the cumulative value of scoring criteria reflects the balance of the positive (vulnerable) and negative (resilient) impacts of climate on a species, with 0 representing a neutral effect. The magnitude of the scores reflects the relative balance of the number of vulnerable and resilient traits possessed by the species for that set of criteria. The overall vulnerability score is scaled to a range of -20 to +20 and each factor or category (habitat, physiology, phenology, biotic interaction) is scaled to a range of -5 to +5. Although the scoring system is based on a linear scale to provide a metric for multispecies comparisons, this does not translate to a linear biological effect of the predictors. In addition, obtaining a maximum or minimum score for a species is unlikely because some criteria only apply to some vertebrate species and traits reflect both resilience and vulnerability. Uncertainty scores should be taken into account when interpreting scores. A high uncertainty paired with a neutral score may indicate a lack of information rather than a realized neutral effect of climate change. Species that receive high uncertainty scores may also be good candidates for further research and monitoring.

Score Applications—Scores can be used to assess individual or multiple species within one or across several target(s). Overall scores can be used to rank vulnerability for a group of species scored for the same target and, along with other considerations, can aid in prioritization, selecting targets for management actions, and planning for climate change. Resilient species can also be targets

for management actions. Multiple scores may also be calculated for a single species at several locations, and across disparate climate projections, to assess relative vulnerability to changes across a broad landscape.

Factor scores highlight the relative contribution of each group of species' attributes (i.e., habitat, physiology, phenology, or interactions) to the vulnerability of one or multiple species to climate change. By highlighting specific areas of concern, factor scores suggest effective areas to target for management actions either by directing management towards an expected source of vulnerability or by identifying common areas of vulnerability for a group of species (Table 5). A strength of SAVS lies in its capacity to identify specific variables relevant to the potential response of individual species to climate change.

Table 5. Examples of management actions that correspond to each of the scoring factors. Many actions can address multiple issues.

Factor	Management Action
Habitat	Manage fire
	Thin forests
	Stabilize stream banks
	Install nest boxes and bat roosts
	Create or enhance corridors
	Translocate individuals or populations
Physiology	Install artificial waters
	Install flood control features
	Protect vegetation types with thermal advantage
	Plant shade plants
	Breed individuals in captivity
	Protect areas with favorable microclimates
Phenology	Line or enlarge water catchments
	Manage areas with different microclimates cooperatively
	Adjust management plans to anticipate shifts in breeding timing
	Maintain important migratory stopover habitat
	Release water from dams strategically
	Take advantage of limiting periods for invasive species control
Biotic Interactions	Provide supplemental food
	Control or reintroduce predators
	Use reintroductions/translocations to replace keystone species
	Reduce opportunities for disease transmission
	Regulate commerce to reduce likelihood of disease introductions
	Control invasive species

USDA Forest Service Gen. Tech. Rep. RMRS-GTR-257. 2011

15

Each question relates to a specific area of vulnerability or resilience and identifies a potential target for management action. For example, if dispersal ability is limited, creation of corridors or translocation of individuals might be used to increase a species' resilience. Uncertainty scores play an important role in identifying research needs or species that will require a more complex assessment of vulnerability.

The application of SAVS scores is limited for some situations. For any species, a single trait or criterion, although equally contributing to the overall score, may represent a critical issue that will lead to population declines despite the presence or absence of other resiliencies or vulnerabilities. Additionally, the scoring system only considers some effects of climate change rather than all possible factors that impact populations. Therefore, scores should be considered within context of each species' biology and current threats in order to gauge future population trends under projected scenarios.

Discussion

We identified 22 criteria predictive of species' response to climate change that, although not an exhaustive list, highlight relevant species' attributes that can be easily and consistently considered across diverse taxa. This scoring system is based on a framework that integrates the three primary aspects of vulnerability, exposure, sensitivity, and adaptive capacity, as well as a measure of uncertainty. Most scoring criteria regard species sensitivity, both with respect to inherent physiological limitations (e.g., low thermal tolerance) and susceptibilities related to behavior (e.g., habitat associations or trophic specialist) (Table 2). Exposure or expected future conditions for a particular region and time period are integrated into the scoring system and results are tailored to the user's needs. A wide spectrum of both direct and indirect climate effects can be accommodated for exposure. Since use of the scoring system relies on the development of a climate change scenario, which identifies future conditions, estimation of exposure can vary among different users and care must be taken to standardize efforts when working in a team setting. Some criteria represent adaptive capacity or potential resilience (Table 2). For instance, dispersal ability and other physiological adaptations that maximize a species' capacity to take advantage of increases in interannual resource variations directly relate to the capacity of species to deal with climate-related changes to habitat. The distinction between sensitivity, exposure, and adaptive capacity have direct relevance to decisions regarding management actions where identifying how a species is

vulnerable to climate change leads naturally to strategies to help that species cope with expected changes or reduce the impact of expected changes (Glick and Stein 2011).

The SAVS was created to provide a straightforward prediction of direction rather than degree of response to reduce scoring variability and ease its use. The SAVS is also flexible to varied and evolving information sources including online natural history databases or personal knowledge. Users can easily recalculate scores as new information becomes available.

Assessments can be used to set conservation goals and engage stakeholders (Füssel and Klein 2008; Glick and Stein 2011). We have used SAVS to assess vulnerability of species for a variety of stakeholders and targeted groups of species in the southwestern United States. Using an earlier version (v1.0) of the tool, we assessed an entire suite of terrestrial vertebrates for riparian forests of the Middle Rio Grande, New Mexico (Friggens and others 2010; Finch and others 2011). Results of this case study were designed to identify and coordinate priority actions across the large number of land managers that oversee this region. Importantly, we found that the greatest vulnerability was associated with not only rare but also relatively common species that generally receive little management attention. We focused on scoring threatened, endangered, rare, and species at-risk for two clearly defined management units, Fort Huachuca and the Barry M. Goldwater Range in Arizona, (Bagne and Finch 2010). Based on specific areas of expected vulnerability along with current threats, we also identified management options, several of which applied to multiple species, such as protecting and enhancing natural or artificial water sources (Bagne and others 2010). Thirty species of conservation interest in the Coronado National Forest, Arizona were targeted for assessment as part of the Forest Service's efforts to integrate climate change into species management plans (Coe and others 2010). As part of this effort, researchers from the University of Arizona created spatially explicit occupancy maps for individual species integrated with vulnerability scores to create maps that outlined hotspots of vulnerability. Although most species expressed some level of resilience to climate change, scores from all assessments indicated greater overall vulnerability for the majority of species, supporting the prediction of challenging times ahead for species conservation. Results also pointed towards relatively large numbers of vulnerabilities in phenology and physiology, which unlike habitat or interactions, are attributes seldom targeted for management and may require more innovative management solutions (Bagne and others 2010).

16

USDA Forest Service Gen. Tech. Rep. RMRS-GTR-257. 2011

Despite uncertainties and because climate change impacts are likely to intensify over time, we need to take immediate action to identify vulnerable species to institute effective management actions and plan proactively. With high likelihood of increasing intensity of warming, even low vulnerability species may be in need of intervention. Assessment is a first step toward anticipating and responding to climate change and SAVS provides a framework for integrating new research and information into species conservation and management planning.

Glossary of Terms and Concepts _____

Definitions for terms and concepts as they relate to SAVS.

1. **Adaptation.** Adjustment or changes in behavior, physiology, and structure of an organism that increase survival or reproduction.

2. **Adaptive.** Exhibiting an adaptation as pertaining to (1) Increased survival or reproduction of an organism (as above) or (2) The process of changing or active learning as in a management decision process.

3. **Adaptive capacity.** The ability of an organism to adjust to changing conditions.

4. **Biodiversity.** The number of genes, species, and ecosystems within a particular area.

5. **Carbon cycle.** The flow of carbon in its various forms through the atmosphere, ocean, and biosphere and lithosphere (IPCC 2007). Carbon dioxide (CO_2), a naturally occurring gas, is the principal greenhouse gas associated with anthropogenically derived warming trends. Sources and sinks within the carbon cycle, along with other greenhouse gases, will ultimately determine atmospheric CO_2 concentrations and the degree of global warming.

6. **Climate.** "Average weather" patterns or trends for a particular region over a period of many years (NCAR 2004).

7. **Climate change.** Change in the state of the climate that is identified by significant changes in the mean and/or the variability of weather parameters and that persist for an extended period, typically decades or longer (IPCC 2007).

8. **Climate projections.** The expected response of the climate system to emissions that are often based on simulations of various emission scenarios and climate models. Climate projections are made with specific assumptions about future emission rates given future socio-economic and technological developments.

Due to these assumptions, projections are considered subject to substantial uncertainty (IPCC 2007).

9. **Climate change scenario.** Projections of climate and related phenomena for the particular region and time period selected by the user for scoring.

10. **Competitive interactions.** Interactions between species to obtain resources in which survival or reproduction are lowered for one species by the presence of another.

11. **Cooperative breeding.** A social system in which individuals care for young that are not their own at the expense of their own reproduction.

12. **Cues.** Indicator used by individuals to signal appropriate or favorable conditions for the initiation of activities.

13. **Critical resource.** Food or other element required for successful reproduction or survival. This may include the availability of certain food items or environmental conditions (rain, calm weather) during critical periods of a species lifecycle.

14. **Disease.** Refers to infectious condition that can be transmitted from one organism to another by direct contact or environmental contamination. Diseases may be caused by viral, bacterial, or fungal organisms. Endo- and ectoparasites may also have the potential to cause mortalities in a population under certain conditions. Climate can affect pathogen and vector population growth, mortality rates, suitable range, and winter survival (Dazak and others 2000; Harvell and others 2002).

15. **Ecosystem.** A system of interacting organisms living in their physical environment.

16. **Endotherm.** Organisms that control body temperature primarily through physiological mechanisms and typically maintain a constant temperature.

17. **Exotherm.** Organisms that control body temperature primarily through external means and generally experience fluctuation in body temperature.

18. **Explosive breeding.** A sudden, concentrated burst of breeding activity that is typically initiated in response to the appearance of some critical resource. This type of breeding is seen in some amphibian species in response to rain events (Wells 2007).

19. **Exposure.** The degree to which a species will experience changing climate and conditions, which will be a function of local climate as well as biology of the species.

20. **Greenhouse gas.** Atmospheric gases (e.g., CO_2, N_2O, CH_4, O_3) that absorb and emit radiation, reflecting heat back to the earth's surface.

21. **Habitat.** The environment naturally occupied by individuals of a species. For scores within the Habitat factor we are referring to habitat type, the particular type of vegetation or aquatic or lithic substrate a species occupies (Morrison and others 1998).

22. **Habitat components.** Discrete physical elements that must be present for a species to reproduce or survive. A habitat component is usually selected by a species at a relatively small scale within the broader habitat type.

23. **Habitat quality.** Feature of occupied habitat that affects rates of reproduction or survival.

24. **Irruptive species.** Species that undergo dramatic, irregular movements (often birds) to areas where they are typically not found.

25. **Management area.** Specific geographical areas administered within a set of defined objectives, generally under a single management entity (e.g., a National Forest, a city preserve).

26. **Microclimate.** Conditions or variations in climate within a small localized area or atmospheric zone. Microclimates are usually influenced by topography, vegetation, structures, or proximity to water and can vary substantially from the general climate of an area.

27. **Mismatch potential.** The risk that a species initiates an activity that is mistimed with an expected or required resource or condition. Climate change can increase the risk of mismatch through three primary mechanisms: (1) changes to a cue upon which a species relies to initiate important biological activities; (2) changes to timing of critical pulses or weather conditions upon which a species relies for successful reproduction and survival; and (3) unequal changes to the timing of cues and resources.

28. **Natural selection.** Differential reproduction or success among groups of phenotypically different individuals (Futuyma 2009).

29. **Nitrogen cycle.** The flow of nitrogen in its various forms through the atmosphere, ocean, and biosphere and lithosphere (IPCC 2007). Nitrogen oxides (NOx) released as a result of soil cultivation practices are powerful greenhouse gases.

30. **Opportunistic breeder.** Species that breed whenever environmental conditions are favorable. Opportunistic breeders depend on short-term factors (cues) such as rainfall, food abundance, and temperature to initiate breeding.

31. **Phenology.** The study of recurring plant and animal life cycle stages (phenophases) such as the leafing and flowering of plants, maturation of crops, emergence of insect, breeding activities, and migration.

32. **Physiological threshold.** Physical conditions beyond which an individual will experience physiological stress that, if sustained, results in death.

33. **Resilience.** The ability to tolerate changing conditions.

34. **Resiliency traits.** Characteristics of species that are expected to increase or not change survival and reproduction, fundamentally or relative to other species. Resiliency is not simply a lack of vulnerability.

35. **Sensitivity.** The degree to which a species is physiologically or behaviorally affected by a particular set of conditions.

36. **Symbionts.** A species that uses an interaction with another species to survive or reproduce. A symbiotic relationship may be mutualistic (benefits both species), parasitic (benefits one species at the cost of another), or commensal (one party benefits and the other is neither harmed or helped). Symbiotic relationships may be obligate (required for the survival of one species) or facultative (beneficial but not required for survival).

37. **Vulnerability.** The state of having increased probability of population decline.

38. **Vulnerability traits.** Characteristics of species that are expected to decrease survival and reproduction, fundamentally or relative to other species

Literature Cited

Adamszewski, J. Z., C.C. Gates, B. M. Soutar, and R. J. Hudson. 1988. Limiting effects of snow on seasonal habitat use and diets of caribou (Rangifer tarandus groanlandicus) on Coats Island, Northwest Territories, Canada. Canadian Journal of Zoology 66: 1986-1996.

Atkinson, C. T., and D. A. LaPointe. 2009. Introduced avian diseases, climate change, and the future of Hawaiian honeycreepers. Journal of Avian Medicine and Surgery 23:53-63.

Araújo, M., W. Thuiller, and R. Pearson. 2006. Climate warming and the decline of amphibians and reptiles in Europe. Journal of Biogeography 33:1712-1728.

Bagne, K. E., and K. L. Purcell. 2009. Lessons learned from pre-scribed fire in ponderosa pine forests of the southern Sierra Nevada. Proceedings of the Fourth International Partners in Flight Conference: Tundra to Tropics:679-690.

Barton, Brandon T, and Oswald J. Schmitz. 2009. Experimental warming transforms multiple predator effects in a grassland food web. Ecology Letters 12:1317-1325.

Beebee, T. J. C., and R. A. Griffiths. 2005. The amphibian decline crisis: A watershed for conservation biology? Biological Conservation 125:271-285.

Beever, Erik A., Peter F. Brussard, and Joel Berger. 2003. Patterns of apparent extirpation among isolated populations of pikas (Oncotona princeps) in the Great Basin. Journal of Mammalogy 84:37-54.

Beissinger, Steven R., J. Michael Reed, Joseph M. Wunderle, Jr., Scott K. Robinson, and Deborah M. Finch. 2000. Report of the AOU Conservation Committee on the Partners in Flight species prioritization plan. Auk 117:549-561.

Bennett, A. F., and J. A. Ruben. 1979. Endothermy and activity in vertebrates. Science 206:649-654.

Benning, T. L., D. LaPointe, C. T. Atkinson, and P. M. Vitousek. 2002. Interactions of climate change with biological invasions and land use in the Hawaiian Islands: Modeling the fate of endemic birds using a geographic information system. Proceedings of the National Academy of Sciences of the United States of America 99:14246-14249.

Bernardo, Joseph, and James R. Spotila. 2006. Physiological constraints on organismal response to global warming: Mechanistic insights from clinally varying populations and implications for assessing endangerment. Biology Letters 2:135-139.

Boag, P., and P. Grant. 1984. The classical case of character release-Darwin's finches (Geospiza) on Isla Daphne Major. Galapagos Biological Journal of the Linnean Society 22:243-287.

Both, Christiaan, Sandra Bouwhuis, C. M. Lessells, and Marcel E. Visser. 2006. Climate change and population declines in a long-distance migratory bird. Nature 441:81-83.

Both, C., and M. E. Visser. 2001. Adjustments to climate change is constrained by arrival date in a long-distance migrant bird. Nature 411: 296-298.

Bowers, J. E. 2007. Has climatic warming altered spring flowering date of Sonoran desert shrubs? The Southwestern Naturalist 52:347-355.

Bradley, N. L., A. C. Leopold, J. Ross, and W. Huffaker. 1999. Phenological changes reflect climate change in Wisconsin. Proceedings of the National Academy of Sciences of the United States of America 96:9701-9704.

Bronson, F. H. 2009. Climate change and seasonal reproduction in mammals. Philosophical Transactions of the Royal Society: Biological Sciences 364:3331-3340.

Brown, James H., Thomas J. Valone, and Charles G. Curtin. 1997. Reorganization of an arid ecosystem in response to recent climate change. Proceedings of the National Academy of Sciences of the United States of America 94:9729.

Butler, R. W. 2000. Stormy seas for some North American songbirds: Are declines related to severe storms during migration? Auk 117:518-522.

Caldeira, Ken, Atul K. Jain, and Martin I. Hoffert. 2003. Climate sensitivity uncertainty and the need for energy without CO_2 emission. Science 299:2052-2054

Carey, Cynthia. 2009. The impacts of climate change on the annual cycles of birds. Philosophical Transactions of the Royal Society: Biological Sciences 364:2231-3330.

Carroll, C. 2007. Interacting effects of climate change, landscape conversion, and harvest on carnivore populations at the range margin: Marten and Lynx in the northern Appalachians. Conservation Biology 21:1092-1104.

Chase, T. N., R. A. Pielke, Sr., T. G. F. Kittel, R. R. Nemani, and S. W. Running. 2000. Simulated impacts of historical land cover changes on global climate in northern winter. Climate Dynamics 16:93-110.

Coe, S., Finch, D., and M. Friggens. (In review) Applying a decision-support tool for assessing vulnerability of wildlife to climate change: a case study on the Coronado National Forest, AZ. USFS GTR.

Coulson, Tim, and Aurelio Malo. 2008. Population biology: Case of the absent lemmings. Nature 456:43-44.

Cowles, Raymond B. 1940. Additional implications of reptilian sensitivity to high temperatures. The American Naturalist 74:542-561.

Crick, H. Q. P. 2004. The impact of climate change on birds. Ibis 146: 48-56.

Daszak, P., A. A. Cunningham, and A. D. Hyatt. 2000. Anthropogenic environmental change and the emergence of infectious disease in wildlife. Acta Tropica 78:103-116.

Dirnböck, Thomas, Stefan Dullinger, and Georg Grabherr. 2003. A regional impact assessment of climate and land-use change on alpine vegetation. Journal of Biogeography 30:401-417.

Dunn, P. O., and D. W. Winkler. 1999. Climate change has affected the breeding date of tree swallows throughout North America. Proceedings of the Royal Society: Biological Sciences 266:2487-2490.

Easterling, D., G. Meehl, C. Parmesan, S. Changnon, T. Karl, and L. Mearns. 2000. Climate extremes: Observations, modeling, and impacts. Science 289:2068-2074.

Eiby, Yvonne A., Jessica W. Wilmer, and David T. Booth. 2008. Temperature-dependant sex-biased mortality in a bird. Proceedings of the Royal Society: Biological Science 275:2703-2706.

Enquist, C., and D. Gori. 2008. Implications of recent climate change on conservation priorities in New Mexico: The Nature Conservancy, Climate Change Ecology and Adaptation Program. 69 pp.

Finch, D. M., M. Friggens, and K. Bagne. 2011. Case Study 3. Species Vulnerability Assessment for the Middle Rio Grande, New Mexico. Pp. 96-103 In: Glick, P., B.A. Stein, and N.A. Edelson, (ed). 2011. Scanning the Conservation Horizon: A Guide to Climate Change Vulnerability Assessment. National Wildlife Federation: Washington, D.C.

Forcada, J., P. N. Trathan, and E. J. Murphy. Life history buffering in Antarctic mammals and birds against changing patterns of climate and environmental variation. Global Change Biology: 14: 2473-2488.

Franklin, Alan B., David R. Anderson, R. J. Gutierrez, and Kenneth P. Burnham. 2000. Climate, habitat quality, and fitness in Northern spotted owl populations in Northwestern California. Ecological Monographs 70:539-590.

Frederiksen, M., F. Daunt, M. Harris, and S. Wanless. 2008. The demographic impact of extreme events: Stochastic weather drives survival and population dynamics in a long-lived seabird. Journal of Animal Ecology 77:1020-1029.

Freed, L. A., R. L. Cann, M. L. Goff, W. A. Kuntz, and G. R. Bodner. 2005. Increase in avian malaria at upper elevation in Hawai'i. Condor 107:753-764.

Friggens, Megan M., Deborah M. Finch, Karen E. Bagne, Sharon J. Coe, and David L.Hawksworth. 2010. Vulnerability of individual species to climate change: Vertebrate species of the Middle Rio Grande Bosque, New Mexico. Report for the U.S. Fish and Wildlife Service created by the U.S. Department of Agriculture, Forest Service, Rocky Mountain Research Station. Report Agreement No. 201819H705. 773 p.

Füssel, Hans-Martin and Richard J. T. Klein. 2008. Climate change vulnerability assessments: An evolution of conceptual thinking. Climatic Change 75:301-329.

Futuyma, D. J. 2009. Evolution, 2nd edition. Sinauer and Associates, Inc: Sunderland, MA. 545 pp.

Gilg, Olivier, Sittler Benoît, and Ilkka Hanski. 2009. Climate change and cyclic predator-prey population dynamics in the high Arctic. Global Change Biology 15:2634-2652.

Gilman, Sarah E., Mark C. Urban, Joshua Tewksbury, George W. Gilchrist, and Robert D. Holt. 2010. A framework for community interaction under climate change. Trends in Ecology and Evolution 25:325-331.

Glick, P., B.A. Stein, and N.A. Edelson (eds). 2011. Scanning the conservation horizon: A guide to climate change vulnerability assessment. National Wildlife Federation, Washington, D.C.: Available: http://www.nwf.org/Global-Warming/Climate-Smart-Conservation/Safeguarding-Wildlife/Assessing-Vulnerability.aspx.

Goth, Ann, and David T. Booth. 2005. Temperature-dependant sex ratio in a bird. Biology Letters 1:31-33.

Grant, R. A. Chadwick, E. A., and T. Halliday. The lunar cycle: a cue for amphibian reproductive phenology? Animal Behaviour 28: 349-357.

Hagan, John M., Trevor L. Lloyd-Evans, and Jonathan L. Atwood. 1991. The relationship between latitude and the timing of spring migration of North American landbirds. Ornis Scandinavica 22:129-136.

Hall, Linnea S., Paul, R. Krausman, and Michael L. Morrison. 1997. The habitat concept and a plea for standard terminology. The Wildlife Society Bulletin 25:173-182.

Hamlet, A., and D. Lettenmaier. 2007. Effects of 20th century warming and climate variability on flood risk in the western U.S. water resources research 43:1-22.

Hannah, L., G. Midgley, and D. Millar. 2002. Climate change-integrated conservation strategies. Global Ecology and Biogeography 11:485-495.

Hargrove, L. J. 2010. Limits to species' distributions: Spatial structure and dynamics of breeding bird populations along an ecological gradient. Dissertation. University of California, Riverside.

Harris, James A., Richard J. Hobbs, Eric Higgs, and James Aronson. 2006. Ecological restoration and global climate change. Restoration Ecology 14:170-176.

Harvell, C. D., C. E. Mitchell, J. R. Ward, S. Altizer, A. P. Dobson, R. S. Ostfeld, and M. D. Samuel. 2002. Climate warming and disease risks for terrestrial and marine biota. Science 296:2158-2162.

Helmuth B., J. G. Kingsolver, and E. Carrington. 2005. Biophysics, physiological ecology, and climate change: Does mechanism matter? Annual Review of Physiology 67:177-201.

Hersteinsson, P. and D. W. Macdonald. 1992. Interspecific competition and the geographical distribution of red and Arctic foxes Vulpes vulpes and Alopex lagopus. Oikos 64: 505-515.

Hitch, A., and P. Leberg. 2007. Breeding distributions of North American bird species moving north as a result of climate change. Conservation Biology 21:534-539.

Holling, C. S. 1978. Adaptive environmental assessment and management. New York: John Wiley and Sons.

Humphries, Murray M., James Umbanhowar, and Kevin S. McCann. 2004. Bioenergetic prediction of climate change impacts on northern mammals. Integrative and Comparative Biology 44:152-162.

Hutto, R. L. 2008. The ecological importance of severe wildfires: Some like it hot. Ecological Applications 18:1827-1834.

Ibáñez, I., J. S. Clark, and M. C. Dietze. 2008. Evaluating the sources of potential migrant species: Implications under climate change. Ecological Applications 18:1664–1678.

Inouye, David W., Billy Barr, Kenneth B. Armitage, and Brian D. Inouye. 2000. Climate change is affecting altitudinal migrants and hibernating species. Proceedings of the National Academy of Science of the United States of America 97:1630-1633.

Intergovernmental Panel on Climate Change [IPCC]. 2007. Climate change 2007: The physical science basis. Contribution of Working Group I to the Fourth Assessment Report of the Intergovernmental Panel on Climate Change. Soloman, S., D. Qin, M. Manning, Z. Chen, M. Marquis, K. B. Averyt, M. Tignor, and H. L. Miller (eds.). Cambridge, United Kingdom and New York, NY: Cambridge University Press. 996 p.

Jackson, Stephen T., Julio L. Betancourt, Robert K. Booth, and Stephen T. Gray. 2009. Ecology and the ratchet of events: Climate variability, niche dimensions, and species distributions. Proceedings of the National Academy of Science 106:19685-196892.

Janzen, Fredric J. 1994. Climate change and temperature-dependent sex determination in reptiles. Proceedings of the National Academy of Sciences of the United States of America 91:7487-7490.

Jenouvrier, S., H. Caswell, C. Barbraud, M. Holland, J. Strœve, and H. Weimerskirch. 2009. Demographic models and IPCC climate projections predict the decline of an emperor penguin population. Proceedings of the National Academy of Sciences of the United States of America 106:1844-1847.

Jiguet, F., A. Gadot, R. Julliard, S. Newson, and D. Couvet. 2007. Climate envelope, life history traits and the resilience of birds facing global change. Global Change Biology 13:1672-1684.

Johnson, Mathew D. 2007. Measuring habitat quality: A review. Condor 109:489-504.

Kearney, Michael, Richard Shine, and Warren P. Porter. 2009. The potential for behavioral thermoregulation to buffer "cold-blooded" animals against climate warming. Proceedings of the National Academy of Science of the United States of America 106:3835-3840.

Ligon, David J., and Brent D. Burt. 2004. Evolutionary Origins In: Ecology and evolution of cooperative breeding in birds. Walter D. Koenig and Janis L. Dickinson (Eds). Cambridge, United Kindom: Cambridge University Press, 292 p.

Lindström, Erik R., Henrik Andrén, Per Angelstam, Göran Cederlund, Birger Hörnfeldt, Lars Jäderberg, Per-Arne Lemnell, Berit Martinsson, Kent Sköld, and John E. Swenson. 1994. Disease Reveals the Predator: Sarcoptic Mange, Red Fox Predation, and Prey Populations. Ecology 75:1042-1049

Lueth, Francis X. 1941. Effects of Temperature on Snakes. Copeia 1941:125-132.

Martínez-Meyer, Enrique. 2005. Climate change and biodiversity: Some considerations in forecasting shifts in species' potential distributions. Biodiversity Informatics 2:42-55.

McCain, Christy M. 2007. Area and mammalian elevational diversity. Ecology 88:76-86.

McCarty, J. 2001. Ecological consequences of recent climate change. Conservation Biology 15:320-331.

Memmott, Jane, Paul G. Craze, Nickolas M. Waser, and Mary V. Price. 2007. Global warming and the disruption of plant-pollinator interactions. Ecology Letters 10:710-717.

Millar, J., and E. Herdman. 2004. Climate change and the initiation of spring breeding by deer mice in the Kananaskis Valley, 1985-2003. Canadian Journal of Zoology 82:1444-1450.

Mitchell, N. J., M. R. Kearney, N. J. Nelson, and W. P. Porter. 2008. Predicting the fate of a living fossil: How will global warming affect sex determination and hatching phenology in tuatara? Proceedings of the Royal Society B: Biological Sciences 275:2185-2193.

Morrison, Michael L., Bruce G. Marcot, and R. William Mannan. 1998. Wildlife-habitat relationships: concepts and applications. 3rd ed. Madison, WI: University of Wisconsin Press. 480 p.

Newton, I. 1994. The role of nest sites in limiting the numbers of hole-nesting birds: A review. Biological Conservation 70:265-276.

Newton, Ian. 2006. Advances in the study of irruptive migration. Ardea 94:433-460.

Parmesan, C. 2006. Ecological and evolutionary responses to recent climate change. Annual Review of Ecology, Evolution, and Systematics 37:637-669.

Parmesan, C. 2007. Influences of species, latitudes and methodologies on estimates of phenological response to global warming. Global Change Biology 13:1860-1872.

Parmesan, C., T. Root, and M. Willig. 2000. Impacts of extreme weather and climate on terrestrial biota. Bulletin of the American Meteorological Society 81:443-450.

Paton, Peter W. C., William B. Crouch, III. 2002. Using the phenology of pond-breeding amphibians to develop conservation strategies. Conservation Biology 16:194-204.

Patt, Anthony G., Dagmar Schröter, Christina A. Vega-Leinert, and Richard J. T. Klein. 2009. Vulnerability research and assessment to support adaptation and mitigation: Common themes from the diversity of approaches. In: Assessing vulnerability to global environmental Change: Making research useful for adaptation, decision making and policy. Patt, Anthony G., Dagmar Schröter, Richard J. T. Klein, and Christina A.Vega-Leiner (eds.). London, UK: Earthscan. 1-26.

Pfennig, D. W. 1992. Polyphenism in spadefoot toad tadpoles as a logically adjusted evolutionarily stable strategy. Evolution 46:1408-1420.

Pike, D., and J. Stiner. 2007. Sea turtle species vary in their susceptibility to tropical cyclones. Oecologia 153:471-478.

Post, Eric, and Nils C. Stenseth. 1999. Climatic variability, plant phenology, and northern ungulates. Ecology 80:1332-1339.

Pough, Harvey F. 1988. The Advantages of ectothermy for tetrapods. The American Naturalist 115:92-112.

Rehfeldt, Gerald E., Nicholas L. Crookston, Marcus V. Warwell, and Jeffrey S. Evans. 2006. Empirical analyses of plant-climate relationships for the western United States. International Journal of Plant Sciences 167:1123-1150.

Rohr, Jason R. and Thomas R. Raffel. 2010. Linking global climate and temperature variability to widespread amphibian declines putatively caused by disease. Proceedings of the National Academy of Science of the United States of America 107:8269-8274.

Root, Terry L , Jeff T. Price, Kimberly R. Hall, Stephen, H. Schneider, Cynthia Rosenzweig, and J. Alan Pound. 2003. Fingerprints of global warming on wild animals and plants. Nature 421:57-60.

Schmitz, Oswald J., Eric Post, Catherine E. Burns, and Kevin M. Johnston. 2003. Ecosystem responses to global climate change: moving beyond color mapping. BioScience 53:1199-1205.

Seavy, Nathaniel E., Kristen E. Dybala, and Mark A. Snyder. 2008. Climate Models and Ornithology. Auk 125:1-10.

Sekercioglu, C. H., S. H. Schneider, J. P. Fay, and S. R. Loarie. 2008. Climate Change, Elevational Range Shifts, and Bird Extinctions. Conservation Biology 22:140-150.

Simeone, A., B. Araya, M. Bernal, E. N. Diebold, K. Grzybowski, M. Michaels, J. A. Teare, R. S. Wallace, and M. J. Willis. 2002. Oceanographic and climatic factors influencing breeding and colony attendance patterns of Humboldt penguins Spheniscus humboldti in central Chile. Marine Ecology Progress Series 227:43-50.

Sinervo, B., F. Méndez-de-la-Cruz, D. B. Miles, and others. 2010. Erosion of lizard diversity by climate change and altered thermal niches. Science 328:894-899.

Skelly, D. K., L. N. Joseph, H. P. Possingham, L. K. Freidenburg, T. J. Farrugia, M. T. Kinnison, and A. P. Hendry. 2007. Evolutionary responses to climate change. Conservation Biology 21:1353-1355.

Stenseth, N. C., A. Mysterud, G. Ottersen, J. W. Hurrell, K.-S. Chan, and M. Lima. 2002. Ecological effects of climate fluctuations. Science 23: 1292-1296.

Thomas, C., A. Cameron, R. Green, and others. 2004. Extinction risk from climate change. Nature 427:145-148.

Tong, Lee and Michael J. McPhaden. 2010. Increasing intensity of El Nino in the central-equatorial Pacific. Geophysical Research Letter 37:L14603-L14603.

Visser M. E., C. Both, and M. M. Lambrechts. 2004. Global climate change leads to mistimed avian reproduction. Advances in Ecological Research 35:89–110

Visser, M. E. 2008. Keeping up with a warming world; assessing the rate of adaptation to climate change. Proceedings of the Royal Society B: Biological Sciences 275:649-659.

Walther, G., E. Post, P. Convey, A. Menzel, C. Parmesan, T. Beebee, J. Fromentin, O. Hoegh-Guldberg, and F. Bairlein. 2002. Ecological responses to recent climate change. Nature 416:389-395.

Walsberg, G. 2000. Small Mammals in Hot Deserts: Some Generalizations Revisited. BioScience 50:109-120.

Wells, K. D. 2007. Mating systems and sexual selection in anurans. In: Wells, K. D. (ed) The Ecology and Behavior of Amphibians. Chicago, IL: University of Chicago Press. p 338-402.

Westerling, A., H. Hidalgo, D. Cayan, and T. Swetnam. 2006. Warming and earlier spring increase western US forest wildfire activity. Science 313:940-943.

Wormworth, J. and M. Karl. 2007. Bird species and climate change; the global status report; a synthesis of current scientific understanding of how anthropogenic climate change impacts on global bird species now and projected future effects. A report to: World Wide Fund for Nature. Sydney: Climate Risk Pty Limited. Available: http://www.climaterisk.com.au/wp-content/uploads/2006/CR_Report_BirdSpeciesClimateChange.

USDA Forest Service Gen. Tech. Rep. RMRS-GTR-257. 2011

21

Appendix 1. SAVS User Guide _____

This is a guide to applying the scoring system developed by the Rocky Mountain Research Station for assessing the vulnerability of individual vertebrate species to climate change (v.2.0). Specifically, these sections provide direction for the inclusion or exclusion of data during the scoring process. We also list suggested sources of information and the type of data that might be helpful for selecting an appropriate response. Reference to literature and italicized terms can be found in the literature cited and glossary sections of the primary document. We recommend documenting sources of information used for scoring as well as explanation of specific score choices. This will aid future edits. Additionally, scores for uncertainty should be noted during the scoring process. Users should make an effort to obtain information for every question, but if response is unknown then assign a score of 0 with uncertainty 1.

Information on projected climate changes for your area of interest should be gathered before scoring species. IPCC (Intergovernmental Panel on Climate Change) reports and Climate Wizard (www.climatewizard.org) are two good starting points for future climate projections. Also consider impacts beyond temperature and precipitation such as flooding, droughts, timing of frosts, wildfire frequency, and changes to snowpack that may affect target species (Table 2). Choose a time period for scoring from available projections that will be relevant to the scope of management planning or conservation needs.

Habitat

H1. Area and distribution: breeding. Is the area or location of the associated vegetation type used for breeding activities by this species expected to change?

Change in area or distribution of suitable *habitat* has a direct impact on populations. Hall and others 1997 defines *habitat* as "the resources and conditions present in an area that produce occupancy—including survival and reproduction—by a given organism." By this definition, habitat extends beyond the vegetation and resources available to an animal. However, for Questions 1 and 2 we are specifically concerned with the resources that provide cover for a species (other aspects of habitat are covered elsewhere) and thus are referring to what may be called *habitat type*: an area supporting a particular type of vegetation or aquatic or lithic substrate (Morrison and others 1998). Consider whether the overall area of the vegetation association for this species' breeding habitat is going to shrink, expand, or move from your targeted area. This question does not require a comprehensive account of all documented breeding locations for an individual species, but the answer should consider all primary vegetation associations collectively where more than one is used regularly. A species is vulnerable to climate change if projections indicate a loss or shift of associated vegetation and resilience to climate change where climate effects are likely to increase the area of a species' associated vegetation type. For geographical shifts, consider your target time period as well as shifts large enough to result in a significant population change (e.g., a shift of >50% from the former range by 2050). There are numerous vegetation classification systems, but most guides and species accounts will report broad biome classifications or biotic communities, which are the most appropriate resolution for this tool. More specific habitat components and resources are considered in other questions.

Relevant data and suggested sources: Information on vegetation associations along with species range is available from most field guides and online species accounts (e.g., NatureServe, BISON-M, Birds of North America Online, AmphibiaWeb). For endangered species, the USFWS recovery plans contain good reviews of available natural history information.

H2. Area and distribution: non-breeding. Is the area or location of the associated vegetation type used for non-breeding activities by this species expected to change?

Species will be impacted by climate-related changes in the area or location of required habitat. Consider vegetation types and habitat associations for the species outside of the breeding season, generally those used in winter. As above, consider geographic shifts within the context of your target time period as well as shifts large enough to result in a significant population change (e.g., a shift of >50% from the former range by 2050). For resident or sedentary species, associations considered here may be identical to those scored in Question 1, in which case the species will receive identical scores for both questions. Stopover or other transitional habitats between breeding and non-breeding habitats are considered in Question 7.

Relevant data and suggested sources: Same as Question 1.

H3. Habitat components: breeding. Are specific habitat components required for breeding expected to change within the associated vegetation type?

Climate change may affect the availability of critical habitat components within primary vegetation types that are required for breeding. Species are vulnerable when climate effects will result in a loss of components and, consequentially, a loss in breeding opportunity. Only specific components or features of the habitat necessary for breeding should be considered (i.e., breeding does not occur without this component). Only components influenced by climate should be considered. Consider whether a required component will become more or less prevalent with changes in climate or related aspects such as disturbance. Examples of habitat elements commonly required for breeding include snags, caves, ponds, rocky terrain (crevices), ice, snowpack, etc. Variation in breeding success associated with a component or habitat characteristic is covered in Question 5.

Relevant data and suggested sources: Field guides or natural history accounts should contain information on required components, if present.

H4. Habitat components: non-breeding. Are specific habitat components required for survival during non-breeding periods expected to change within the associated vegetation type?

Climate change may affect the availability of critical habitat components that are required for survival rather than reproduction as in Question 3. Only specific components or features of the habitat necessary for survival during non-breeding periods should be considered here. Components may be a physical feature, such as a cave for hibernation or may be directly related to climate, such as snowpack, but components must be required elements for species' occurrence rather than to improve survival (Question 5). Other examples of habitat components necessary for survival include flowing water, subnivean space (Coulson and Malo 2008), and anything that provides protection from harsh weather conditions and is absolutely required for species survival. Consider whether a required component will become more or less prevalent with changes in climate or related aspects such as disturbance.

Relevant data and suggested sources: Information regarding habitat components, if present, is readily available in most species' natural history accounts or online species accounts.

H5. Habitat quality. Within the habitats occupied, are features of the habitat associated with better reproductive success or survival expected to change?

Habitat features associated with quality are those that incur variation in survival or reproduction. These can be aspects of habitat components (Question 3 and 4). Consider aspects of the habitat (e.g., vegetative cover, snow depth)

that directly lead to differential breeding or survival success in the focal species and that will ultimately affect populations. Do not consider changes in overall habitat availability (area), the presence or absence of critical habitat components, or direct impacts to food resource availability. Examples of habitat features sometimes related to quality include: ash deposition in water sources or increased erosion from increased fire activity (associated with lower quality), less forage due to reduced ground cover (lower quality), shrub density, water temperature of ephemeral ponds, and presence of forest mosaics (versus homogenous stands) (see Johnson 2007 for discussion). Consider whether projected changes in climate conditions will increase, decrease, or not affect habitat quality. Habitat quality may not be relevant for many species and habitats (particularly ephemeral habitats such as early serial stages of vegetation) where differences in structure or element composition are of minimal importance to the perpetuation of a species. Where relationship of habitat quality with climate projections is unclear, score as 0 with a 1 for uncertainty. Food resources should be considered under Biotic Interactions.

Relevant data and suggested sources: Habitat quality is often discussed in reference to locations with variable fitness or in reference to habitat selection. Additionally, references may refer to sources and sinks: source populations are locations where recruitment exceeds mortality and sinks are where recruitment does not exceed mortality. Indicators of habitat quality include (1) the rate of species survival and reproduction, (2) species fecundity, and (3) length of time a habitat is suitable for residence by a species (Morrison and others 1998). Information on quality of habitats is sometimes listed as part of natural history information, but more often it needs to be checked within the wider scientific literature. Research related to quality will not be found for all species. Aspects related to quality may also be included as part of conservation strategies for the species. Try a query including "quality" or "habitat selection" and the species name in a scientific database (e.g., Google Scholar, BIOSIS). Also try a query using species name and "winter" or "mortality."

H6. Ability to colonize new areas. What is the potential for this species to disperse?

Species that are able to readily disperse are likely to be able to travel to new locations if needed and, thus, are considered more resilient to potential habitat changes. Consider species' capacity to move to new habitats or favorable microclimates both within the context of the selected time period of climate projections and the magnitude of

USDA Forest Service Gen. Tech. Rep. RMRS-GTR-257. 2011

23

the changes. Species that only move long distances over several generations may not have the capacity to respond to rapid climate-mediated changes in habitat. Sex-biased dispersal (i.e., dispersal by only one sex) or strong site fidelity will counter some of the benefits of mobility. Site fidelity or territoriality restricted to the breeding season would not constitute inability to disperse for this question as its effect is only temporary. Dispersal may also be limited by barriers, including those that are physical, behavioral, or physiological, that effectively decrease the realized dispersal of a species. When movement to alternative suitable habitats is likely inhibited by one or more such barriers, then dispersal should be considered limited and the species vulnerable. In other instances, barriers may neither hinder nor help dispersal and the user should score the species according to its innate capacity to move long distances.

Relevant data and suggested sources: If species' mobility is not known, data on species' range, average dispersal distances, presence of sex-biased dispersal, maximum known dispersal, or homing capacity are useful. Studies of the effect of habitat fragmentation may provide useful to assess a species' capacity to move to new locations. Look for information in species accounts and life history papers. NatureServe often provides further discussion regarding dispersal abilities and barriers in its species accounts. Knowledge of the geographic features of the focal scoring area is useful to judge whether geographic barriers may be an issue. Finally, information regarding the expected shift in habitat (e.g., 300 m upslope in 50 yrs) may be useful for providing a measure by which to assess species' dispersal capacity.

H7. Migratory or transitional habitats. Does this species require additional habitats during migration that are separated from breeding and non-breeding habitats?

Species that require additional habitats beyond breeding and non-breeding (e.g., wintering grounds) sites may be more vulnerable to climate effects, because we cannot expect parallel changes in all these habitats. Good examples of species with additional habitat requirements are long distance migratory birds that require stopover sites to replenish resources as they move between breeding and wintering sites. Some mammal species also migrate across long distances through transitional habitats. Whenever additional habitats are geographically distinct and subject to different climatic changes or comprised of different vegetation types a species should be considered vulnerable. Distance alone, however, may not determine

whether a species uses transitional habitats. Species that move through transitional habitats without resource utilization such as long distance migratory birds that have non-stop flights or elevational migrants that shift flexibly over relatively short distances, are not considered vulnerable to this effect.

Relevant data and suggested sources: Basic natural history information should contain migratory information. Specific stopover information, which is often unknown, is not required for scoring. A basic climate projection map or vegetation map should indicate if transitional habitats are separate from breeding and non-breeding habitats.

Physiology

PS1. Physiological thresholds. Are limiting physiological conditions expected to change?

Species often exist near their physiological limits with respect to temperature or moisture tolerances. If projected future conditions increase the likelihood that a species will experience limiting conditions (high heat, desiccation), then the species will be vulnerable to climate-related population declines as habitat becomes unsuitable for species survival. Alternately, some species may benefit (exhibit increased resilience) when projected changes predict a move away from currently limiting thresholds as might be found for a cold sensitive species under a warming scenario. Consider both minimum and maximum thresholds of the focal species and, when both are likely to be influenced with distinct outcomes, select the variable that is most limiting for survival when scoring. For instance, in cases where a species may be limited by temperature maximums but benefit by changes in temperature minima, base the score on the limiting effect; here it is the maximum temperature. Species that have moderate thermal range tolerances that are rarely exceeded under future scenarios or are able to avoid limiting conditions (e.g., aestivators) are not considered physiologically vulnerable to climate changes and are given a neutral score (option b) unless that species is also expected to experience a decline in the incidence of lower thresholds, in which case option c should be selected. In general, species that currently tolerate very hot conditions along with those known to be intolerant of high temperatures may be vulnerable (Bernardo and Spotila 2006; Jiguet and others 2007). Species that require moist conditions and are prone to drying (e.g., many amphibians) will be vulnerable to both temperature and precipitation changes.

Relevant data and suggested sources: Information may be limited to laboratory experiments, which do not directly correspond to survival in the field. If not directly

24

USDA Forest Service Gen. Tech. Rep. RMRS-GTR-257. 2011

reported, a number of substitutes may be used to infer whether a species exists near its temperature or moisture threshold. Demonstrations of recent population shifts or records of die-offs during extreme weather may indicate physiological limits. Range boundaries available in basic species accounts often indicate a climatically driven limitation and thus species living along the boundary of their range are likely near their physiological limits. Also, location of species within its distribution (e.g., populations of interest at southern limit of range or only occur in moist microsites), or the range of thermal conditions (e.g., species that occupy areas of limited variability or that occupy extreme environments may have narrow tolerances), may be informative for predicting species distribution. If no prediction can be made, score as 0 but also uncertain.

PS2. Sex ratio. Is sex ratio determined by temperature?

Some reptile species are known to have temperature-determined sex ratios. Consider the effect of temperature on sex determination and whether future climate conditions may favor one sex over another. Although there have been some examples in other taxonomic groups with differential survival of embryos with temperature, this effect has generally not been well studied. There is some evidence that temperature can influence sex ratio in other taxa, such as birds and mammals, though this is not due to temperature-dependent sex determination but to other effects such as differential mortality or hormonal changes (Goth and Booth 2005). Differential mortality in young through temperature dependent mechanisms can lead to population declines if the effect is strong enough (Eiby and others 2008). If temperature has a sex-biased effect on survival of offspring, only consider situations where this effect is likely to result in strongly skewed sex ratios across populations.

Relevant data and suggested sources: This trait can usually be found in natural history profiles, field guides, or species accounts.

PS3. Exposure to weather related disturbance. Are disturbance events (e.g., severe storms, fires, floods, etc.) that affect survival or reproduction expected to change?

This question regards mortalities caused by disturbance events. Extreme weather events that may change under future scenarios and are known to cause massive population declines in a variety of taxa include droughts, unusually low or high temperatures, freeze/thaw events, false springs, storms (rain, ice, snow), heavy snowfall, and heat waves (Parmesan and others 2000; Easterling and others 2000).

To be considered vulnerable, a species' population should experience significant mortality as a direct result of the disturbance event and those events should be projected to increase. Do not include indirect effects of these events on resources (see Biotic Interactions) or habitat (see Habitat). Do consider the frequency, timing, and duration of these events when choosing a response. Consider the impact of disturbances for both breeding and non-breeding periods and again choose the most limiting condition when multiple effects are expected. For migrants, breeding and non-breeding may be in separate regions and have different projections. For non-migratory species, differences may simply be seasonal. Evidence of past response to extreme weather conditions relating to heat waves and drought are better used to inform decisions regarding physiological thresholds (Question 1) rather than this question.

Relevant data and suggested sources: Gather information on species habitat from natural history accounts or field guides and consider it in relation to your climate projection information. Population studies may be additionally helpful as they consider events related to mortality. Look for observed cases of mass mortality related to disturbances, as these are often unusual enough to inspire documentation.

PS4. Limitations to daily activity period. Are projected temperature or precipitation regimes that influence activity period of species expected to change?

Activities important for survival or reproduction may be limited by environmental conditions and result in increased species' vulnerability. Often limitations are associated with high temperatures or dry conditions, but they can also be limited by cold or snow. Specifically consider whether the projected changes will lead to increases or decreases in activity periods that have the potential to affect survival or fecundity. Diurnal species may be exposed to greater temperature extremes, but nocturnal species may be less tolerant of extremes. Crepuscular species may already be restrained in an active period and unable to shift to nocturnal or diurnal activities. Ectotherms may be more vulnerable, because they rely more on behavior to adjust to changes in ambient conditions (Kearny and others 2009; Sinervo and others 2010).

Relevant data and suggested sources: Some useful information should be available in general natural history information. Look for information on limiting conditions for activity and timing of active periods and consider how these conditions may be altered. Most information on activity will be available on foraging or resting behaviors, but consider if these have the potential to affect fitness.

USDA Forest Service Gen. Tech. Rep. RMRS-GTR-257. 2011

25

PS5. Survival during resource fluctuations. Does this species have alternative life history pathways to cope with variable resources or climate conditions?

Some species have alternative life history pathways or employ strategies that allow them to maximize reproduction and survival under variable conditions, which is likely to confer resilience to expected climate changes. Focus should be on issues related to expected increases in climate variability, thus interannual, rather than intrannual, variation. Beneficial traits may be morphological or behavioral and can include the ability to take advantage of years with good conditions or the ability to cope during years with poor conditions. Species that undergo irruptive migrations, undergo explosive breeding events, use cooperative breeding systems, or can employ alternate phenotypes (e.g., neotony, carnivorous phenotypes) are examples of animals that have coping strategies which allow them to deal with resource variation and shortages. Species that are able to delay breeding altogether (prudent parent) (see Forcada and others 2008), fertilization (e.g., some snakes, insects, others), or implantation (e.g., marsupials, some mammals) may also have an advantage if the trait improves long-term productivity. Conversely, a species without flexible strategies or with strategies that are not expected to increase its ability to survive during periods of low resource levels is considered vulnerable.

Relevant data and suggested sources: Life history/species accounts will generally list alternative life history pathways and often include information related to the advantages of these strategies. Consider your regional projections and how the identified alternatives may or may not be advantageous.

PS6. Energy requirement. What is this species' metabolic rate?

Mark as appropriate. Ectotherms (e.g., lizards, frogs) have the lowest metabolic requirement, about 1/10 the energy of endotherms (Pough 1988). Metabolism in endotherms (e.g., mammals, birds) is considered moderate for this purpose unless known to be particularly high relative to other vertebrates, such as in hummingbirds or shrews.

Phenology

PH1. Mismatch potential: cues. Does this species use temperature or moisture cues to initiate activities related to fecundity or survival?

Cues may initiate activities such as migration, ovulation, egg laying, or emergence from hibernation. Cues can be exogenous (e.g., day length, lunar cycle) or endogenous (e.g., rise in body temperature, circadian rhythm) (Grant and others 2009). Exogenous cues are also often linked to climate conditions such as time since frost, mean minimum or max temperature, and the initiation of a rainy season. Species that rely primarily on a cue related to temperature or precipitation to initiate activities will be more likely to experience impacts related to changes in timing. Species that rely on endogenous rhythms or cues are not subject to this risk. A score indicating vulnerability should be reserved for those species where a change in climate leads to a change in the timing of a distinct cue and thereby the initiation of a major life stage (e.g., emergence from aestivation/hibernation, migration). This does not include smaller scale adjustments where species delay or shorten the timing or duration of certain activities (e.g., egg laying, incubation periods) in response to ongoing weather conditions, as these are unlikely to result in population change.

Relevant data and suggested sources: Life history/species accounts should list activities. How a species times activities is not always included in these accounts, but it should be available from more general information on taxonomic groups or on the timed activity such as migration.

PH2. Mismatch potential: event timing. Are activities related to species' fecundity or survival tied to the availability of discrete resource peaks (e.g., food, breeding sites) that are expected to change?

Variation in the timing of critical resources due to climate change leaves species at an increased risk of mistiming their activities and species with such dependencies are considered more vulnerable. Assess if the species relies on a discrete resource event limited in time such as the emergence of insects or flowering plants. Certain weather conditions may also be discrete events that may be important such as calm weather for successful bird migration or onset of rainy season for amphibian breeding activity. If these periods are likely to change, then the migrating species is likely to be negatively impacted. Not all resources or favorable conditions will be limited to discrete time periods or will be affected by projected climate change.

Relevant data and suggested sources: You first need information on what discrete events are important for your species and should be available in life history/species accounts. You will then need to consider if the timing of these events is affected by climate or climate-mediated criteria. For this you may need additional information regarding resource pulses and/or biological properties of prey/forage species, which could be provided through accounts created for those species. Observations related

26

USDA Forest Service Gen. Tech. Rep. RMRS-GTR-257. 2011

to annual variation in fitness or behaviors often hold clues to possible events of importance. The presence of a climate mediated timed event is sufficient evidence for vulnerability and you are not required to estimate the magnitude of the timing change.

PH3. Mismatch potential: proximity. What is the separation in time or space between cues that initiate activities and discrete events that provide critical resources?

Indicate whether a species initiates activities immediately in response to or in the immediate vicinity of a changing critical resource. The probability of a mismatch between initiating an activity and a critical resource increases with the length of time or distance between events. For instance, the rate and degree of climate changes are likely to differ between temperate and tropical zones and between upper and lower elevation sites, with consequences for species migrating between these areas (Both and Visser 2001). Long distance migrants may be less able to respond to climate changes because of the disjunct between the effects occurring at their breeding grounds versus non-breeding grounds (Crick 2004; Wormworth and Mallon 2007; Carey 2009). In some instances, there could be a fairly constant level of critical resources that would make a timing mismatch unlikely. Opportunistic breeders and irruptive species are good examples of animals that respond directly to a resource pulse. Other species are unlikely to respond within a short period of time to changes in resources, such as those whose activities are initiated in different latitude, time zone, elevation, or habitat type from critical resources.

Relevant data and suggested sources: Life history/ species accounts and information gathered for the previous two questions is applicable here. You may need additional information regarding resource pulses and how they are affected by climate. Timing of flowering, insect emergence, and temporary water sources are known to be influenced by climate and can be applied to scoring generally without more detailed information.

PH4. Resilience to timing mismatches during breeding. Does this species have more than one opportunity to time reproduction to important events?

The ability to breed multiple times a year increases the chances that at least one of those attempts is optimally timed with resources. Indicate how species' reproductive period is distributed within a single year. Species need to breed and produce young more than once to qualify as resilient (i.e., a species that re-nests within a constrained

period of time should not be considered to be resilient).

Relevant data and suggested sources: Life history/species accounts should have this information. Avoid using rare cases to determine score.

Biotic Interactions

The following questions require some knowledge of climate change effects on interacting species that have some demonstrable influence on the species under study. Strong interactions are relatively rare in most species and so the additional research required for this section will often be minimal. However, in the case where there is a notable or influential relationship between species, understanding how climate impacts will affect both parties is critical to assessing species vulnerability. Indeed, such a relationship may be one of the most important determinants of vulnerability.

I1. Food resources. Are important food resources for this species expected to change?

Consider important foods and especially any resources that are critical for species survival even if that resource is only required for a limited period. When an important resource has been identified, consider broadly how projected changes in climate are expected to impact this resource. Climate may reduce food resources by causing a shift in vegetation communities. Alternatively, population crashes of important food resources (see Parmesan and others 2000 (insects), Stenseth and others 2002 (fish), others) due to climate extremes or extreme weather events (storms) or disturbances (disease, fire) can also occur. If the species utilizes several food sources with variable potential responses to climate change projections, then (b) will be the most appropriate selection. Consider whether food resources may be limited during critical periods such as during reproduction or migration.

Relevant data and suggested sources: Diet is most commonly reported in natural history documents although it is not always well documented for individual species or across a species' range. A score of 0 is appropriate where information is absent. Most applications of this potential vulnerability will be those with more specialized diets, but some food resources may also be predicted to change even if comprised of multiple species. Life history and species accounts may provide information on potential direction of change for an animal species used as a resource. Additional information on a taxonomic group of interest may be found with online scholarly search engines such as Google Scholar or BIOSIS.

USDA Forest Service Gen. Tech. Rep. RMRS-GTR-257. 2011

27

I2. Predators. Are important predator populations for this species expected to change?

Only predator species with a demonstrable impact on populations should be considered. If there are several predators with varying expected responses to climate change projections, then we assume that overall predation effects will remain unchanged. Climate could also affect the intensity or impact of predation without changes in the size of predator populations (e.g., loss of cover). When this impact has a strong potential to affect a species' population, it is appropriate to count this as a predator-related vulnerability. No prediction is made if mortality from predation is low.

Relevant data and suggested sources: Life history/species accounts. A general understanding of the potential response of predator species to projected climate changes is required. This will likely involve reviewing the natural history of the predator or doing a literature search.

I3. Symbionts. Are populations of symbiotic species expected to change?

We define symbiotic relationships to include any type of required interaction with another organism(s). Consider species that are part of an obligatory mutualism (required for survival or breeding), commensalism, or parasitism (i.e., the focal species is parasitic). If the symbiotic species is only a food resource and already considered in Question 1, then score as 0 here unless there is some additional aspect to the relationship that has not been addressed.

Relevant data and suggested sources: Life history/species accounts should list the presence of a symbiotic species. Knowledge of symbiont life history characteristics and potential response to climate change projections may be required (see Question 2). This question does not apply to hosts of parasites (see Question 4).

I4. Disease prevalence. Is prevalence of diseases known to cause widespread mortality or reproductive failure expected to change?

Consider only those pathogens or parasites that are known to cause substantial mortality or loss of fecundity. In addition to the disease-causing agent, consider how climate affects the incidence, spread, or virulence of the disease. Vector-borne diseases may be particularly prone to range expansions if climate projections alter range suitable for vector populations. For any disease or disease agent, vulnerability is associated with an increased mortality that occurs as a result of exposure to new diseases through introductions or range expansion or increased incidence and severity of diseases already affecting the species that may occur due to increases in vector populations. Disease incidence may also increase as warmer temperatures reduce cold related die-offs and extend activity period of both pathogens and their vectors. Resilience is associated with a decrease in mortality through any of these types of mechanisms. Climate changes can also indirectly affect disease spread through increases in crowding if resources become more limited (e.g., shrinking water sources) or by increasing host susceptibility (e.g., body condition or resistance is reduced). Consider crowding only when there is a demonstrable relationship between crowding and disease outbreak (e.g., many water borne pathogens) as well as mechanism where crowding is expected to increase (e.g., concentration of limited water sources).

Relevant data and suggested sources: Life history/species accounts should provide information regarding disease susceptibility. USGS National Wildlife Health Center is a good source of wildlife disease information, and a field manual of bird diseases is available online (http://www.nwhc.usgs.gov/publications/field_manual/). Literature searches of the species name or family and "mortality" may also be helpful. In addition some diseases may have detailed projections related to climate change, particularly if they affect human health as well (e.g., malaria). Primary literature search of the specific pathogen with reference to climate change or range expansions is recommended. For any significant diseases, follow up with a search for transmission risk factors.

I5. Competitors. Are populations of important competing species expected to change?

Criteria: Consider the effects of climate changes on competing species that displace or negatively affect survival or reproduction in the species of interest. Specifically, note whether major competitors, those that are known to outcompete a species, will benefit or not by projected changes in climate. Consider introduced as well as native species.

Relevant data and suggested sources: Information on important competing species is often included with information on species conservation. Suggested control measures may indicate if certain climate conditions favor these species.

The Rocky Mountain Research Station develops scientific information and technology to improve management, protection, and use of the forests and rangelands. Research is designed to meet the needs of the National Forest managers, Federal and State agencies, public and private organizations, academic institutions, industry, and individuals. Studies accelerate solutions to problems involving ecosystems, range, forests, water, recreation, fire, resource inventory, land reclamation, community sustainability, forest engineering technology, multiple use economics, wildlife and fish habitat, and forest insects and diseases. Studies are conducted cooperatively, and applications may be found worldwide.

Station Headquarters

Rocky Mountain Research Station
240 W Prospect Road
Fort Collins, CO 80526
(970) 498-1100

Research Locations

Flagstaff, Arizona	Reno, Nevada
Fort Collins, Colorado	Albuquerque, New Mexico
Boise, Idaho	Rapid City, South Dakota
Moscow, Idaho	Logan, Utah
Bozeman, Montana	Ogden, Utah
Missoula, Montana	Provo, Utah